07 2021

DISCARD

RECOVERING FROM YOUR CAR ACCIDENT

The Complete Guide to Reclaiming Your Life

James F. Zender, PhD

ROWMAN & LITTLEFIELD
Lanham • Boulder • New York • London

This book represents reference material only. It is not intended as a medical manual, and the data presented here are meant to assist the reader in making informed choices regarding wellness. This book is not a replacement for treatment(s) that the reader's personal physician may have suggested. If the reader believes he or she is experiencing a medical issue, professional medical help is recommended. Mention of particular products, companies, or authorities in this book does not entail endorsement by the publisher or author.

Published by Rowman & Littlefield
An imprint of The Rowman & Littlefield Publishing Group, Inc.
4501 Forbes Boulevard, Suite 200, Lanham, Maryland 20706
https://rowman.com

6 Tinworth Street, London SE11 5AL, United Kingdom

British Library Cataloguing in Publication Information Available

Library of Congress Cataloging-in-Publication Data
Names: Zender, James F., 1954- author.
Title: Recovering from your car accident : the complete guide to reclaiming your life / James F. Zender, PhD.
Description: Lanham : Rowman & Littlefield, [2020] | Includes bibliographical references and index.
Identifiers: LCCN 2020009910 (print) | LCCN 2020009911 (ebook) | ISBN 9781538133972 (hardcover) | ISBN 9781538133989 (epub)
Subjects: LCSH: Traffic accidents—Psychological aspects. | Traffic accident victims—Rehabilitation.
Classification: LCC RC1045.P78 Z46 2020 (print) | LCC RC1045.P78 (ebook) | DDC 363.12/514—dc23
LC record available at https://lccn.loc.gov/2020009910
LC ebook record available at https://lccn.loc.gov/2020009911

This book is dedicated to all of the survivors of vehicular trauma and their families who have allowed me the privilege of traveling with them on their roads to recovery and taught me much about surviving trauma, thriving, and life.

RECOVERING FROM YOUR CAR ACCIDENT

CONTENTS

FOREWORD

"There could be swelling in your brain and you could lose consciousness at any moment and slip into a coma. You could also become paralyzed within the next half hour," the paramedic replied when I asked if it was really necessary to strap me to a board and put me in a neck brace. I looked back briefly at the wreck of the car we had just been in. In that moment, the overwhelming exhilaration I had felt from surviving the crash was replaced by the most crippling fear I'd ever known. What if within minutes I would lose the ability to stand or walk? What if these were my last moments of consciousness, or even the last moments of my life?

The night before had been one of the most amazing nights of my career. I performed Ireland's rugby anthem to a large stadium audience with hundreds of thousands watching live and on TV. The following afternoon, a friend offered to give me a ride to the airport. Attempting to merge into an exit lane on the highway, he swerved across two lanes of heavy traffic and lost control of the car. We were traveling at 50 mph. I grabbed on to the dashboard as the car flew off the road, up into the air. This is it, I thought. We are all going to die. I was shocked to think that this is how my life would end.

To escape the overwhelming assault of surreal horror, my very being seemed to curl in on itself, into a tiny corner of my mind, as though I were trying to hide. We hit a lamppost. Everything went black. I came to as the car rolled and my head hit hard on the roof. Piercing high-pitched screams from the backseat punctuated the sound of breaking glass and crunching metal. We were upside down. My head hit hard on the roof once again as I glimpsed the green of the grassy ditch. I don't know how many times the car rolled, but I remember my head hitting with intense force on the roof, several times. The car finally came to an angled stop on an embankment, facing the opposite direction of the traffic. There was just enough room for me to open the passenger door. All three of us in the car were injured.

I was first diagnosed in the hospital emergency room with a mild concussion, along with neck and back soft tissue injuries, and had horrible bruising on my legs. The attending physician cleared me to fly and advised me to see my family doctor once I returned home. I assumed this meant I would be fine once I got some sleep and the bruises faded.

Three wheelchairs, one long flight home to London, replete with a panic attack and vomiting, difficulty standing in one spot as well as walking, dizziness, a constant headache, mental fog and confusion, two dreadful car journeys, sharp stabbing head pains, and several hours of coma-type sleep later, I ended up back in the hospital emergency room. I was then diagnosed with postconcussion syndrome, told that brain swelling and a possible bleed could still occur, and advised not to go back to work for at least a few weeks.

In the ensuing days and months, I had difficulty keeping my balance and walking up and down stairs. I often couldn't understand what people were saying and struggled to be around more than one person at a time. I couldn't lift a pot or prepare simple meals. I had difficulty dressing, applying makeup, and washing my hair. My short-term memory was practically nonexistent. I would buy apple juice four times in one day because I forgot that I had already been to the store and bought some. I was afraid to go to sleep for fear I would slip into a coma and die. My nights were a mixture of passing out from intense exhaustion to having insomnia and horrible nightmares. Train, bus, and taxi rides to and from doctors' appointments became the most frightening, exhausting experiences.

Several times in the first few months, I was told that I wasn't yet out of the woods as there was still a chance of a brain hemorrhage. I suffered through constant anxiety, panic attacks, flashbacks, and debilitating depression. Emotionally, I relived every trauma I had ever experienced as if it were happening all over again. I was then diagnosed with a TBI (traumatic brain injury), PTSD, and depression, on top of my soft tissue injuries. A plethora of prescriptions for painkillers, brain stimulants, and antidepressants were prescribed. I often wished I had died in that car. I wondered why I was still alive. It was no kind of existence. Beyond appearing tired all the time, I looked completely normal, and no one seemed to understand what I was going through.

My world became a long, lonely, challenging journey of recovery with more than 16 doctors, therapists, and specialists in two different countries. I battled relentless fatigue and always felt like a zombie, constantly trying to get my brain to wake up. I couldn't handle much light, noise, or too much stimulation. I had difficulties communicating to friends, family, and colleagues. I was most comfortable alone in a quiet, dark room listening to relaxing, guided, self-healing meditations and taking baths. I couldn't handle simple arithmetic or basic transactions. When I was better able to hold a pen, I found that my handwriting was a sloppy mess, despite my utmost concentration on shaping each letter.

In the six plus years since the accident, no one has had any conclusive answers for me on how long to expect my remaining PTSD and brain injury symptoms to continue. I do know that I will forever live with chronic pain in both my neck and back.

I have had to learn to take control of my own recovery and not to rely solely on the expertise of doctors and therapists. I have undertaken alternative treatments and research on vitamins, read and listened to others' stories of recovery, and spent countless hours sifting through Google searches for answers.

I recently discovered the wonderful, inspired work and writings of Dr. James Zender. His *Psychology Today* blog on motor vehicle accident trauma and brain injury is extremely insightful, compassionate, and comprehensive. We connected on Twitter as mutual admirers of each other's work. I was delighted when asked if he could interview me for his blog and if I would write the foreword for this book. I am honored to assist in helping to introduce you, the reader, to a book that I believe will lend a much-needed form of support, care, knowledge, and practical information for all of those affected by motor vehicle accidents, brain injury, and PTSD.

Motor vehicle accidents and the resulting injuries do not discriminate based on age, gender, socioeconomic status, culture, ethnicity, or on any other basis. Too many motor vehicle accident survivors live with the stigmas attached to having invisible disabilities, as is the case with brain injury, chronic pain, and mental health conditions. Sadly, there is no tested and true road map for much of the recovery process. Researchers still have so much to uncover about the effects of injury to the brain and the complexities of trauma on the human psyche and the body. Most TBIs will not show on a CT scan or an MRI, but that doesn't mean that damage isn't present.

Within the current healthcare/medical and legal systems that should protect, nurture, nourish, and care for us, fear is all too pervasive. It is amazing that even with so many incredible advances in social and medical technology over the last 50 years, antiquated systems continue to subsist that cater to the lowest common denominator, our most primitive, animal-based needs.

There is great fear of what we have yet to fully understand about ourselves physically and emotionally, fear of helping another at the cost of one's own time and/or resources, fear of being faced with our own and others' mortality, and fear of people malingering or being dishonest solely for monetary gain from insurance companies that are set up for capital gain, as opposed to helping injured individuals. What is the value of a healthy, pain-free human life? Why must we as survivors fight to make our pain known, to be believed, and to fight for treatments and support on top of suffering from grave injuries?

I have learned that it is what breaks, within our minds, our spirits, and our bodies, that not only makes us stronger but also makes us human. Our physical and emotional pains can act as gifts, and can provide a rich context within which to deepen our bonds of connection to ourselves and to others. The new foundation we are forced to build after traumatic injury allows us to grow, often times into even better versions of ourselves. We have the power to become beacons of light and inspiration. I have discovered that our bodies and our spirits have an immense capacity for healing and overcoming obstacles when we give more love, compassion, and understanding to ourselves, and to others. Our healing is aided when we find a willingness to create a new way of being, practice humility, show vulnerability, ask for help, and learn to accept our limitations. We discover new strengths, yet must constantly tweak and redefine our new post-injury reality. Healing and living with disabilities provide a constant reminder to cherish and have gratitude for simply being alive. It is often through tragedy and trauma that we gain clarity on life's purpose. We are here on this planet to help one another to survive, to thrive, to love, and to be loved.

We can and must rise above base mentalities. We need more conscientious healers and beings who are willing to explore—to ask questions, practice closer, deeper communications with others, and create a more comprehensive, holistic modality of moving forward after an accident. We need more knowledgeable advocates that believe it's worth the effort to undertake more research, and mend the current systems in order to better deliver the needed care and therapies. As car travel is a necessity, we need higher safety standards for vehicle manufacturers, as well as more accident-prevention efforts. We need continued faith in a higher power and constant reminders to take life one day at a time. We need more wonderful therapists like Dr. Zender, with a dedication to healing, knowledgeable and empathic doctors and specialists, as well as immensely supportive family, friends, and pets.

We survivors, and all of those affected by the devastation of motor vehicle accidents, are in dire need of Dr. Zender's comprehensive guide to help us explore our new inner worlds, adjust to and accept our post-injury selves, further understand our injuries and what to expect in the recovery process, and navigate the challenging, complex world of the current medical/legal systems. Dr. Zender's efforts provide light and hope, and serve as a reminder that we are truly not alone on our road to recovery. Please find comfort, support, and a wealth of knowledge in this incredible book.

With love and sincerest wishes
for your best health and happiness in this life,
Angela Nielsen-Molineux

PREFACE

Nearly 90 years ago, my mother, then age four, and her sisters were celebrating the Fourth of July with firecrackers when my Mom's chiffon dress caught fire. She sustained third-degree burns on her body and face. Incapacitated from her injuries for six months, she came close to losing her young life. As time went by, her physical scars paled in comparison to her internal, emotional disfigurement. A light in her mind had switched off, and whether alone or with others, an impenetrable darkness hung over her. Whenever she met a new acquaintance, she felt compelled to explain the deep gouges on her chin. Once, during a conversation with her, I unconsciously rubbed my chin. She thought I was mocking the scars on her face and launched into a brutal emotional attack.

The trauma from my mother's horrible childhood tragedy overshadowed her life and then mine. Every Fourth of July, my loving mother experienced rages that chilled me to the bone. During those terrifying and heartsick episodes, I tried but failed to restore her. I carried the burden that her despair was my fault. While all my friends' families celebrated the holiday by filling the sky with rainbows of light, in my home there was only joyless darkness.

Decades passed before I came to understand that my mother's rages were not my fault. Her rages were a result of the thundercloud of her trauma, which always lingered. In a twist of unfortunate fate or unconscious orchestration, I was born into this world late in the evening on the third of July. My mother seemed to hold me responsible for the firecracker that came close to taking her life. Instead of a celebration, my birthday marked a gloomy kickoff to the Fourth, reminding my family of the terrible pain and scars that would forever haunt my mother and leave her feeling insecure.

To me, she was beautiful and the facial damage was insignificant. Her disproportionate reactions and the abuse she aimed at my father and me were confusing. What had I done to deserve such treatment? I hadn't even been born when the tragedy occurred almost a century before.

It was a miracle my mom survived her injuries as she received no hospital care. It was the early 1930s in a small town in central Ohio. The town doctor made daily house calls while my grandmother lovingly nursed my mother back to health. My mother was the strongest, hardest-working woman I have ever known, despite her dark episodes and battle with mental illness. My father was equally hardworking, and his commitment to our family through so many difficult times is something I will always admire and respect him for.

It's April 1, 2019. I now sit at a writing desk in a home created by the famous architect Louis Le Vau. I consider how many years he spent designing the Palace of Versailles for the French king Louis XIV. Built in 1645, the house sits on Ile Saint-Louis, a picturesque island on the Seine, in the heart of Paris not far from Notre Dame.[1]

I am here at an international neurology and neurosurgery conference to speak about pain and topics related to auto-accident traumas and have extended my stay to work on this book. The writing desk is a long, wooden table in a redesigned kitchen that's nestled in a stone, vaulted basement.

The walls and arched ceilings consist of stones set in place more than 350 years ago by masons whose skills are long lost to the winds of time. This ancient home (or "hotel," as it was called in France) has been wonderfully preserved and updated to become a luxurious home.

How strange. Immediately after writing the above words about this magnificent house, I receive a text message from the owner. He writes that he was struck by a car as he rode his bicycle on a New York City street and is now on heavy pain medication for his injuries. His tragic accident is an all-too-common occurrence in this age of speeding drivers or drivers distracted by high-tech gadgets like cell phones. Pedestrian and bike accidents are on the rise, and the injuries resulting from automobile versus human are often severe, if not fatal. We can tumble from fortunate to disabled in an instant.

Just three weeks ago, I said my final goodbye to my mother as she took her last breath. It had been two years since she'd moved in with my family. Surviving a severe illness had left her frail, yet she outlived my father and nearly her entire cohort. She passed away in her grandson's bedroom shortly past midnight, after a day of receiving all of our support. Her process of letting go of her 91-year-old body was agonizing for all of us.

My decision to get away from life in Michigan in order to grieve and process her passing also afforded me the time and focus needed to complete this book. Until Paris, my writing had been difficult given that my clinical and family demands left me little time or energy. An abrupt change was needed, and Paris in April was just what the doctor ordered. My final nudge to Paris was the invitation to be a conference keynote speaker.

An amazing experience, the conference allowed me to meet new friends and colleagues from around the world, all engaged in clinical and scientific work. One fascinating lecture was presented by a biochemist from Saudi Arabia. She spoke about her research on the brain-gut connection in autism and the use of probiotics as a treatment. What neurotrauma might be related to the autistic brain, and what could be done to restore its functioning?

This book, which I have been working on for the past four years, received its inception in a Harvard Medical School Continuing Education course on writing and publishing in healthcare. Directed by Julie Silver, MD, the 2015 course transformed my professional life. I came to see the vital necessity of creating a book about my work with auto-accident survivors—a subject I have been immersed in for the past 15 years.

The countless stories of survivors' ordeals trouble me, and I know we can do better in their treatment. Auto accidents are a global pandemic causing more than one million deaths, and 50 million injuries and disabilities each year. Most people have sadly become numb to these commonly occurring traumas that threaten to kill or disable us and those we love.

This book raises awareness of the significant public health risk of auto accidents with the resulting brain, body, and psychological traumas, and the possibilities for prevention. In 2019, I was honored to be a guest faculty member at Dr. Silver's course to discuss my experience writing this book. It is my dream to teach at Harvard and to have the opportunity to educate and influence 300 Ivy League doctors and professionals about issues in auto-accident trauma care that they might not have heard about—for example, Michael D. Lewis, MD's Omega-3 protocols for treating brain injury. (Lewis was an army physician who discovered the effectiveness of high doses of fish oil in treating and preventing severe brain injury.)

As my subspecialization in trauma has become increasingly known in the Detroit area, I receive one to two, or on rare occasions three to four, new auto-accident patient referrals daily. Many of these patients suffer from symptoms of post-traumatic stress, depression, anxiety, panic attacks, sleep disorders, pain disorders, and traumatic brain injuries.

My scope of practice helps these patients understand—through education, support, direction, and encouragement—that they are *not* going crazy, but that something crazy *has happened to* them. Their coping skills have often been overwhelmed, and guidance in rebuilding or finding new skills is a necessity. I help family and friends comprehend a survivor's difficulties with thinking, speech, mood, sound, light, and relationships. Often, referrals to other medical experts are needed—specialists who, like me, can help see the scorpion while viewing the snake.

In 2019, I was at an international traumatic stress conference in Washington, DC, where I gave a poster presentation on chronic pain and accident trauma. While talking with an expert in PTSD, it shocked me to hear that they'd only seen two or three auto-accident patients in their long academic and clinical careers. Their confession stunned me, as auto accidents are the number one cause of PTSD. Hearing this firsthand from an icon in the field further supported my belief that we need an entirely separate diagnostic category for the constellation of psychological, neurocognitive, and neurobehavioral symptoms reported after auto-accident trauma. The constellation of these symptoms results in what I refer to as Motor Vehicle Trauma (MVT). I suggested MVT as a syndrome in my *Psychology Today* blog, which made Healthline's list of Best Traumatic Brain Injury Blogs in 2019.

I realize that a similar set of symptoms can result from accidents in other kinds of transportation, such as sailboats. However, we are not exposed to sailboats to the same degree that we are to cars, trucks, buses, and motorcycles. Perhaps the constellation of symptoms could be referred to as *Moving* Vehicle Trauma.

President Abraham Lincoln's wife, Mary Todd Lincoln, suffered a brain injury from a carriage rollover. Along with the tragedies of seeing her husband assassinated, suffering the loss of two young children, and living through the Civil War as the First Lady, did the carriage accident also contribute to her mental illness? Did her infamous extravagant spending stem from the impulsivity and the compromised judgment we frequently see in frontal lobe damage that results in impaired executive functioning?

As a result of my *Psychology Today* blog, I came in contact with a former Special Forces, Green Beret, Andrew Marr, who wrote a book about his post–traumatic brain injury. Written with his brother Adam Marr, *Tales from the Blast Factory* chronicles Andrew's mental and physical decline following deployments in Afghanistan and the failed efforts of the VA system to restore his health.

Mark L. Gordon, MD, wrote Marr's foreword. Gordon saved Andrew from dissolving into a soup of neurobehavioral and neuroemotional dysregulation. Andrew's brain injury resulted from exposure to explosive combat shock waves. The blast-induced neurotrauma impacted his endocrine system, which affected his hormonal and metabolic functioning and led to Andrew's deteriorating cognitive and behavioral functioning as well as depression.[2]

Dr. Gordon practices interventional endocrinology and has achieved impressive results in the treatment of survivors of traumatic brain injuries in both military and civilian cases. He uses protocols that include hormone replacement therapy and nutraceuticals. I have read testimonials from patients who have regained their lives because of his procedures based on blood testing and close clinical monitoring of treatment responses. For Andrew, Dr. Gordon's protocols resulted in dramatic, rapid, and sustained improvement.

Dr. Gordon's and others' opinion that PTSD may be a manifestation of a damaged brain has increasingly convinced me that we do a disservice to our patients when we do not consider the possible role of a neuroendocrine dysregulation as a root cause of symptoms. The brain may be damaged from inflammatory responses in need of repair, and all the psychotropic medications in the world will not address this damage. According to the testimonies of Gordon's patients, protocols that target reducing neuroinflammation have been key. Gordon refers to supporting the body's ability to recover by creating a neuro-permissive environment that facilitates neuroplastic repair of brain structure and functioning.

As I move through life as a clinician, I am continually confronted with new findings that change everything in terms of how I think about and approach my work. My views on psychotherapy are perpetually evolving and under revision. The needs of those who come to me for treatment and help on their healing journeys are always on my mind. Much of what is believed today will be proven wrong tomorrow. As Joseph Campbell once said, "The best we can do is lean toward the light."[3] We can only strive to do our best.

Most everyone agrees that prevention is a hard sell. Since the invention of the automobile, a staggering number of related deaths and injuries have had a devastating impact on the global economy because of medical costs and lost productivity. The pain, suffering, and lowered quality of life could fill an entire ocean.

Society has accepted the cost of lives and limbs due to our love of this mode of transportation. I find it interesting that discussions of massive opiate-related deaths are compared to auto-accident deaths and used as a horrifying benchmark. Americans are more likely to die from an accidental opioid overdose than from a car accident.[4] I wonder how many of the opiate-related deaths were auto-accident survivors who were prescribed opiates to treat chronic pain from their injuries.

As I revisit this preface in March 2020 while the whole world is turned upside down amid the clutches of the Covid-19 pandemic, I find it interesting to hear the president of the United States comment that the number of automobile accidents is far greater than the number of cases of the often deadly virus.[5] Perhaps once the world recovers from its current crisis, more attention will be given to the daily threat of auto-accident injury.

As a child, I was taught Benjamin Franklin's adage, "An ounce of prevention is worth a pound of cure." As a society, we need to focus on preventing auto-accident injuries. Can we do better in our efforts? I think so.

This book gives voice to the survivors of auto-related collisions. My gratitude goes to my patients who allowed me the privilege of guiding them on their journeys to recovery after having survived accidents on the roads. They are the experts of vehicular trauma, and from them, we must learn. Stories taken from patients and composites of patients, highlight core themes of the auto-accident recovery experience and process. I have also included stories of non-patients who shared their trauma recovery experience with me. Their accounts provide an additional layer, and they too have nurtured my commitment to this book, for which I am much appreciative.

Many said it would have helped significantly to have had a written road map to recovery after their accidents. There were few directions to find their way back to who they were before the incident. I attempt to allow them to speak to you through these pages. It is their voices that must be heard.

We have learned much about trauma and its impact on both the body and the mind since my mother's tragic childhood accident. Her trauma shaped her life, which in turn shaped mine and led to my decision to become a psychologist. There was no one to really help her through the physical, mental, and emotional pain that she endured. Had there been, much suffering could have been avoided. It is my hope that this book will help to reduce the suffering of auto-accident survivors so that they, and their children, will not have to bear the heavy burden of the many ghosts of trauma.

Dr. James Zender
Paris, France

ACKNOWLEDGMENTS

I'd like to extend my heartfelt thanks and immense gratitude to the multitude of wonderful people who helped to make this book possible. All of your incredible contributions and support have greatly assisted my lifelong dedication to helping trauma survivors recover.

I'd like to begin by thanking my late parents, Reva and Joe, for exemplifying resilience in overcoming trauma and major adversity and providing me with the inspiration to pursue clinical work in the area of trauma. Thank you to Marie, Kate, and Nick, my loving family, who kindly gifted me with an atmosphere of peace and solitude for weeks on end as I slaved away at my desk. I could not have completed this book without your love and support!

My deep appreciation and gratitude as well to William and Phylis Bauer for their long dedicated friendship.

I could not have started this book without the initial encouragement and excellent directional tools from Dr. Julie Silver. I deeply appreciate her support through the moments when I felt like giving up.

I owe huge thank-yous to my writing coach Lisa Tenner and my writing accountability partner Dr. Gayle Myers for their much-appreciated encouragement and moral support.

I'd like to thank Dr. Alan Robertson who introduced me to the world of auto-accident trauma and whose knowledge and support made all the difference.

I'm eternally grateful for the excellent guidance and mentorship I received from my agent Linda Connor. Thank you for believing in this book and finding the right publishing house. To everyone on my publishing team at Rowman & Littlefield, I'm hugely grateful for your support. In particular, I'd like to thank Suzanne Staszak-Silva for her patience, attention to detail, and invaluable input throughout my writing process.

From the book's inception to completion, I continued to have a full clinical practice. My amazing assistant Eliza Foksinski was absolutely invaluable in orchestrating all aspects of preparing this book and kept everything running smoothly. Thank you!

Special thanks to my amazing personal trainer, Magda Sadowski, who kept *me* running smoothly and was instrumental in helping me maintain optimal physical and mental health. Just don't tell her that the odd glass of Macallan on the long, late nights of writing helped too! A big thanks as well to Jesus Alfredo Perez and Satbir Singh who kept my car well tuned!

I truly don't know where online I would be without my fantastic social media guru Frances Caballo who connected me to the global MVT/PTSD/TBI community. Thank you, Frances.

I was so blessed to have the immense editing talents of Robbie Sommers Bryant, who often worked virtually with me through the night. She was always awake and would respond almost instantly, even if I e-mailed her at 3 a.m. Thank you so much, Robbie! I'd also like to give a special heartfelt thank you to Angela Molineux for writing a brilliant foreword and carrying this book across the finish line with her inspired editing skills.

I am forever grateful to the many knowledgeable individuals who lent their remarkable contributions. I have to give a huge shout-out to both Dr. Mark Gordon and Andrew Marr for their inspiring work, encouragement for this book, and groundbreaking contributions to the field of trauma and TBI treatments. I'd also like to thank producer/director Jerri Sher for her excellent work on the documentary *Quiet Explosions*. I'm especially thankful for Dr. Bessel van der Kolk. His pioneering work on psychological trauma has been an inspiring, guiding light to me for many years. I must thank the late Dr. Krystal, also of real inspiration to me, for his mentorship in trauma work.

Much gratitude to Professor Jay Fienman, Esq., whose insightful book *Delay, Deny, Defend* shined a spotlight on insurance law and gave me the knowledge that allowed me to touch on some important legal issues in my book. I'd also like to express my thanks to James Mangraviti Jr. Esq. for his excellent medicolegal courses and wise personal counsel along with other members of the legal community for giving me their valuable time and educating me on the relevant legal issues pertaining to patient recovery.

Thank you to the following pioneers in the study of the impact of road traffic trauma on the body and mind: Doctors Edward J. Hickling, Edward B. Blanchard, Diane Poole Heller, Lawrence S. Heller, and Peter Levine. Much appreciation and thanks as well to Dr. Martin E. P. Seligman who led the profession of psychology in a healthy direction.

This book would not have been possible without the helpful insights and contributions from my patients. I'm extremely grateful to them for granting me their trust in the therapeutic process and expanding my awareness of their conditions and the trauma recovery process.

I'd like to give tremendous thanks to the first responders, emergency personnel, doctors, therapists, and all of the treatment providers who dedicate their lives to assisting and treating automobile crash survivors. I'm much obliged to the auto insurance and legal professionals whose diligent and often valiant efforts help to ensure that patients have adequate coverage and access to treatment.

It's been a pleasure over the years to contribute to *Psychology Today*. Many blessings and thanks to the editors for supporting my efforts and publishing my blog on overcoming psychological trauma.

Much appreciation and thanks as well to the following individuals for their contributions and support: Aleida Lucena, Magda Sadowski, Linda Anger, Rusty Shelton, Martha Murphy, John Hanc, Kelly Mallone, Jeanne Marie Laskas, Dr. Michael Meeron, Dr. J. Alan Robertson, John Gwynne Prosser, Dr. Martin Wunch, Dr. Debby Feinberg, Wendy Lavin, Dr. Jeffrey Eisman, Dr. Dan Farkus, Dr. Emad Alatassi, Dr. Joe Lupo, David J. Morris, Dr. Jessie Lupo, Dr. Jeff Lupo, Belleruth Naparstek, Dr. Mitchell L. Clionsky, Dr. Richard Klein, Dr. Bruce H. Lipton, Kristin Priest Sokul, Dr. Robert Farhat, Dr. Robert Pohl, Dr. Ivete C. Fernaz, Travis Mills, Dr. Gabor Mate, Dr. Sylvie Lombardo-Pohl, Timothy Hoste, Dr. Alicja Poleszak, Barie Shaqiri, Dr. Tejpaul Pannu, Kevin McKinney, Dr. John N. Briere, Dr. Thomas Spoon, Dr. Charles R. Figley, Dr. Timothy Wasmund, Dr. Anthony Pulice, Tory Hudson McDonald, Dr. Bradley G. Sewick, Dr. Richard Weiss, Tom Constand, Rhonda Westphal, Dr. Opada Alzohaili, Dr. Charles Seigerman, Matt Friedman, Angie Williams, Dr. Craig Ross, Dr. Anthony Petrilli, Dr. Candace B. Pert, Ramonda Walker, Sandy Mabry, Dr. Michael Lewis, Cheryl Palmer, Jessica Couch, Donna Parks, Dr. Clark Elliott, Ann Brainard, Meredith Look, Jodi Coden, Margaret Kammerer, Joel Legree, Kary Barnard, Sierra Leone Donaven, Dr. Michael Kapsokavathis, Saphira Linden, Dr. Chris McNeil, Kathleen Dunning, Betsy S. Green, Dr. Robert M. Sapolsky, Thomas Watkins, Nancy Harshfield, Montell Williams, Dr. Joe Dispenza, Christopher Felton, Dr. C. B. Scrignar, Mary DuPrie, Saphira Barbara Linden, Karen Baird, Michael N. Hough, Robert M. Whitehead, Dr. Herbert Benson, J. J. Virgin, Deborah Feinberg, Liz Neporent, Deborah Powell, Diana Armstrong, Sandy Smith, Cathy Grochowski, Dr. Joseph Tafur, Carie Wright, Robin Silas, Anna Trela, Any Dubey, Jason Groth, Steve Hart, Jody B. Lipton, Esq., Dee Hamka, Sofia Allar, Matthew Payne, Esq., Dr. Stanislav Grof, Dr. Ana Lucia Nicastri, Dr. Pat Ogden, Kathryn N. Kunst, Anna S. Allar, Nicole Ulrich, Mary McRae, Jason Barbaro, Jayne Janes, Lawrence Lewis, Steven Kotler, and countless others who have contributed in various ways—many thanks!

Last but never least, I must not forget to thank my dogs Molly and Teddy who spent many hours by my side, lending their patience and emotional support!

INTRODUCTION

This book, written primarily for the recovery of a car accident survivor, is intended to help those who've been injured—as well as their families, friends, employers, and insurance and legal professionals—gain new insights and understanding regarding postaccident stressors, symptoms, conditions, and treatment issues. I will attempt to address the top four main questions asked after an auto accident: What is happening to me (or my loved one)? What should I do? Where should I go? What can I expect from therapy?

For most people, it's difficult to understand what's not been directly experienced or felt. Because of this fundamental truth about human nature, empathy for others is often in short supply. It is my hope that this book will increase understanding of the Motor Vehicle Trauma (MVT) experience, amplify empathy for the suffering of its victims, stimulate new and better ways of helping to restore balance and wholeness in the lives of those affected, and expand professional awareness of the impact of MVT to lead to earlier interventions. Increased awareness can and will help to prevent more significant impairment, compromised living, and lower quality of life.

As a survivor reading this book, you will acquire strategies for living with chronic pain; coping with post-traumatic stress disorder (PTSD); and dealing with a traumatic brain injury, depression, sleep disturbance, and anxiety. Through their stories, other survivors will teach you how to cope with the impact of your injuries on family and social relationships and come to terms with a period of compromised functioning and disability, both temporary and in some cases permanent.

You will learn how to reach out for support from family members, friends, support groups, and/or professionals, and how to help others understand your challenges. You will find ways to heal and to achieve the best recovery. You may also discover new meaning in your life and a renewed life purpose through your recovery efforts and struggle with pain.

The following pages provide a road map for recovery and offer hope and direction from others who have traveled the same overwhelming and perplexing path you now find yourself on. You will

1. meet more individuals who have been injured and are finding ways to manage and overcome their emotional and physical afflictions.
2. observe that both individual and group psychotherapy have helped survivors understand and manage their distressing, confusing, and anxiety-provoking symptoms.
3. learn to accept and love yourself as a whole person again, even if you don't feel like the person you were before the crash.
4. gain hope that with the right guidance, direction, support, and team, you may find yourself on a path that's even better than the one you were on before you were injured.

More broadly, this book is also intended for all the other people who play roles in the auto-accident drama, including the following:

1. Parents preparing their teenage children for the excitement of the driving experience, the growing independence that driving signifies, and the dangerous risks involved in handing the keys over and letting an adolescent drive.

2. Emergency medical service personnel and the hospital emergency department physicians and staff, as well as healthcare treatment providers. (Thorough diagnostic evaluations and accurate documentation can mean the difference between life and death, and later, how the crash survivor is treated by insurance professionals and the legal system.)
3. The policy makers with the power to institute systems and policies that can reduce the risk of car accidents and increase roadway safety.
4. The designers and manufacturers who should consider the psychological impact of the injuries that can result from accidents in the vehicles they place on the roads.

The issues that result from car accidents are vast and could fill many books. However, few address the many layers of recovery or the complicated voids intertwined with the physical/psychological damage from a collision.

We live in a world impacted by the worldwide public health crisis of auto-accident trauma. Post-traumatic stress disorder occurs more frequently as a result of car accidents than war, yet the academic world of trauma research has predominantly focused on the aftereffects of war. Perhaps this stems from a collective PTSD form of denial because cars are everywhere, they are familiar, we use them every day, and we cannot escape the carnage. Interesting that the word "car" is in the word "carnage."

Professional trauma researchers have focused on military, and to a lesser extent, natural disaster trauma. Precious few books have been written on auto-related injuries, yet hundreds focus on war trauma, domestic violence, and rape trauma. An intensely traumatic event that can often haunt a car-accident victim forever has mainly been neglected.

For the past 30 years, I have worked as a trauma psychologist helping people with every imaginable form of trauma. It has been a privilege to see countless people learn to cope, heal, move on, and transform from their traumatic incidents. We live in a world of joy and horror. Unfortunately, those touched by the horror and brushed by death often become blind to the joy. To survive and thrive in this world, we must balance experiencing both joy and horror, Yin and Yang.

For the past 15 years, my Detroit-based practice has become a center for the psychological care of people injured in auto accidents. Through the commonalities in treating hundreds of patients who have survived automobile wrecks (involving every form of motorized vehicle), I have recognized what I call Vehicular Trauma Syndrome (VTS). This syndrome consists of a constellation of physical, psychological, cognitive, emotional, social, occupational, family, and legal factors.

From what I have witnessed in my practice, quality of life can be stripped away in an instant after an auto accident and can take months, years, or a lifetime to regain. Even so, it is possible for you and your loved ones to escape the terrifying feelings of isolation, to accept your postaccident life, and to begin the sometimes long journey to recovery.

TRAUMATIC BRAIN INJURY: A SILENT EPIDEMIC

This book is heavily skewed toward the presentation of issues related to traumatic brain injuries. The brain is particularly vulnerable to subtle and sometimes not-so-subtle injuries from the mechanical forces of an auto accident. Along with being a clinical and forensic psychologist, I am also a brain injury specialist certified by the American Brain Injury Association. My work and interests are focused on the neuropsychological injuries that often result from car-related trauma. I am fascinated with the workings and misworkings in the brains of auto-crash survivors and witness brain injuries in my clinical office practice daily.

Unfortunately, when a collision results in a brain's inability to work correctly, the injured person often is unaware of it. They may simply think that they're not feeling "like themselves." They rarely connect their uncomfortable experience to the brain trauma. Friends and family members may not be aware of these changes or may not want to acknowledge them. However, when the evidence piles up from countless examples of compromised cognitive and emotional functioning, everyone must come to the often frightening conclusion that something is wrong. Examples may include the following:

1. Chronic forgetfulness.
2. Severe and unremitting fatigue.
3. Sleep disturbances.
4. Uncontrolled temper.
5. Laughing or crying spells.
6. Impulsivity.
7. Having difficulty organizing oneself or one's work.
8. Chronic headaches.
9. Vision and hearing changes.
10. Tinnitus.
11. Speech problems, stuttering, or stammering.
12. Light and sound sensitivity.
13. Dizziness, balance problems, and nausea.
14. Problems reading or doing math.
15. Temperature dysregulation.
16. Weight gain or loss.
17. Changes in menstrual functioning.

These are symptoms that must be medically and psychologically investigated to determine the root cause so that appropriate treatment can be provided.

Separately, any of these symptoms may be significant but not signs of injury to the brain. Yet, I often see many of these symptoms manifesting in the collective as a ruthless consequence of car crashes. The symptoms usually represent the result of some trauma to the brain.

Because brain injuries are so often undiagnosed, not recognized, or neglected in people who have sustained car-crash injuries despite the devastating impact these injuries can have on quality of life and functionality in all areas, my book emphasizes this "silent epidemic."

Brain injuries are generally overlooked when the symptoms of auto-crash survivors are first diagnosed. Insurance companies do not welcome and do not like to consider neurotrauma. Even professionals who are aware of and routinely treat people with brain injuries are often insensitive and dismissive of the challenges the condition presents. For example, the huge packets of medical paperwork and legal forms that patients are presented with are often extensive and overwhelming and can threaten to swallow survivors like quicksand. Patients will be dismissed from practices because they miss too many appointments due to forgetfulness or anxiety about leaving the house. The attorneys who represent them are upset by their poor judgment and impulsive behavior. Judges do not understand or factor in symptoms of a brain injury that may dictate behavior. Most people with brain trauma would benefit from qualified, dedicated, and actively involved case managers who can assist with filling out paperwork, making and keeping appointments, and coordinating necessary care.

We do not live in a brain injury–sensitive world. My hope is that this book will help to raise awareness of the needs and difficulties faced by people who suffer brain trauma from car accidents.

This book stays close to my visceral experience as a clinician treating hundreds of car-accident survivors. We live in an era of the buzz expression "evidence based," which has a politically correct implication that academic policy makers demand. The information and my recommendations herein are based on my direct clinical observations of what happens, what works, and what doesn't work for surviving and thriving after severe, auto-accident related trauma.

I have included many of the stories of survivors in this book in the hope that you might identify with and take comfort from knowing that you are not alone in your journey to recovery.

If you have a traumatic brain injury, or are currently struggling with chronic pain or fatigue, I recommend you take rest breaks as you read this book. You may also like to take notes on tips you find helpful.

1

LIFE AFTER YOUR MOTOR VEHICLE TRAUMA

I am not what happened to me. I am what I choose to become.
—Carl Gustav Jung[1]

You've survived a horrific car accident. You're happy to be alive, but it feels like your whole world has shattered in a split second. It may feel like you've been transported to another planet where you're drowning in a sea of pain and heightened emotion. You may begin to notice new, frightening symptoms in the weeks following the accident, and you may no longer feel like the person you once were. Maybe you and your loved ones have noticed changes in your behavior and abilities. You might begin to wonder if you will ever get back to fully living and enjoying life.

I have written this book to help you successfully set upon and navigate the complex path to reclaiming your life. I will help you to identify and understand your physical and psychological injuries; discover management and treatment options, including alternative treatments for the most common auto-accident injuries; and identify the key legal and healthcare professionals who can assist in your recovery.

Billions of people around the globe are affected directly or indirectly by roadway collisions. For the past several years, auto-accident fatalities in the United States have exceeded 40,000 *each year.* At that current rate, 800,000 people will die in the next 20 years. Every year, approximately 2.9 million people in the United States sustain auto-accident injuries, which often become lifelong disabilities.

The stories I hear from my patients typically begin in a quiet, routine way. They were driving home from work, mulling over a project of the day, or thinking about what shopping needed to be done to entertain relatives for the Labor Day weekend. Or maybe they were enjoying a leisurely weekend road trip with their family. Then suddenly, seemingly out of nowhere, *crash!* Shattered windows. Shattered bones. Shattered lives. Shattered plans. The search for a new normal—life after the devastating collision—begins.

At the start of your recovery, statistics probably do not interest you. You just want to stop hurting and return to work—to your preinjury style of living. You want your life back. Through discovering that your injury experiences are similar to others in this book, you will realize that you are not alone.

The aftereffects of a crash can be overwhelming: chronic pain, depression, anxiety, panic attacks, insomnia, and post-traumatic stress disorder (PTSD). Changes in personality as a result of a brain injury and coping with pain can make living a quality life difficult or impossible. Survivors often experience problems in their careers and personal relationships, and many develop mental health conditions as a result of their injuries. The life trajectories of survivors and their loved ones are often altered, sometimes permanently.

MARILYN'S STORY

When Marilyn first came to see me, she was depressed, angry, and in pain. While making a delivery for her job, another vehicle slammed into the side of her car. After the collision, Marilyn continued with her just-push-on-through approach to life. But in the weeks that followed, she noticed growing pain in her neck, back, right knee, and progressively, throughout her body. She realized that the unremitting pain took a toll on her work, and the ability to focus on the minute details of her job was diminishing. A continual cramp in her head and neck, which required repeated stretching, haunted her. She reluctantly agreed with her primary doctor's suggestion to obtain a medical leave of absence from work while she attended to her rehabilitation.

Eventually, specialists diagnosed injuries to the vertebrae of her neck. Due to her global pain indicators, she was also determined to have fibromyalgia. The persistent discomfort disrupted her sleep and left her in an endless state of exhaustion. Her pleasant nature spiraled into depression. Increasingly irritable and, at times, aggressive, Marilyn soon preferred to be alone, and she withdrew from friends and family.

"It was as though all my anger and anxiety bubbled through and caused a domino effect in my life. I'm not the same person. When my neck pain is at its highest, no medication works, and nothing calms down the pain. Having no relief, I get frustrated, scared, and angry."

Marilyn became emotional to the point of aggression, and on several occasions, it reached a crescendo when she physically abused her family. "Somewhere along the way, I crossed a line," she said. "I had what I consider a 'breakdown.'"

Eventually, Marilyn underwent neck surgery. Her physical pain was reduced, which allowed her to become more active in individual and group therapy. Slowly, she picked up the pieces of her life. She began to smile more. Repairing relationships damaged by the anger generated by her constant pain became her focus. Surgery helped, but it didn't solve all of her problems. For Marilyn, the support she received through psychotherapy was key to her regaining a sense of her pre-injury self.

KALIE'S STORY

Kalie's story is slightly different from Marilyn's. After being rear-ended in a hit-and-run on the freeway, she received excellent care from a team of specialists. As she began the healing process, her doctors realized she'd likely suffered a traumatic brain injury (TBI) from the high-speed impact. She received an extensive neuro-psychological evaluation that confirmed a diagnosis of TBI and began specialized therapy to help her manage problems with her memory and speech. She was also diagnosed with post-traumatic stress disorder. Once she learned how the ordeal had affected her, she became better at handling excessive irritability, chaotic emotions, and jumbled thoughts that threw her off-balance in her relationships.

Kalie cannot imagine where she'd be if she hadn't found the right team of doctors to guide her recovery. "Without help to process the pain, injuries, and rejections," she said, "you become a shell of a person. Once you have an auto accident, you're not living a fulfilling life at that moment. Recovery doesn't happen overnight. You have to learn patience."

The first gift she received, she said, were the doctors who showed empathy and care and understood the problems she was having. The second gift, which she gave to herself, was her willingness to accept that she had been injured, allowing her to open the door to healing. Deciding to not only attend individual psychotherapy sessions but also to join group therapy sessions once a week was a significant turning point for her. Group therapy helped her move from a sense of isolation to a feeling of acceptance by connecting with others who were familiar with her challenges and experiences.

Group therapy is one place where you might find an abundance of healing. Something almost magical happens after auto-accident survivors come together. Once they share their experiences and realize others are suffering similar symptoms, they often say the weight of the world lifts from their shoulders. The fear of being "crazy," which trauma survivors commonly face, often evaporates. I will highlight all of the extensive benefits of group therapy in chapter 10.

Through group and individual therapy, Kalie came to see her traumatic experience as an opportunity to learn, grow, and make life improvements. Practicing gratitude and being open to challenging your previously held views and values are ways you can inspire hope within yourself.

CHRONIC PAIN—THE MIND-BODY CONNECTION

One significant challenge you may confront in your recovery is chronic pain. Your suffering can seem like a well of dejection from which there is no salvation.

The Greek physician Hippocrates recognized the mind-body connection more than two thousand years ago. Increasingly, Western medicine is relearning to honor and harness this knowledge. It's as if mind and body merge into a two-way mirror and reflect what is happening in each.

Through the mind-body connection, both Marilyn and Kalie discovered that regulating their emotions helped with pain management. Taking charge of the pain lessened the feeling of being a victim of the pain. The ability to acknowledge, express, and process their emotions allowed them both to heal, regain some sense of control over their lives, and increase involvement with their family and others.

OVERCOMING A FEELING OF ISOLATION

In 1990, I became the founding director of the Center for the Prevention and Treatment of Psychological Trauma at Detroit Receiving Hospital. It is one of the busiest trauma hospitals in the world where the top trauma surgeons perform medical miracles every day. Thousands of cases of shock and injury come through the doors.

During my time there, I had the privilege of being mentored by several pioneers and leaders in psychological trauma. I drew upon their expertise in my efforts to develop a world-class trauma center in the turmoil-filled streets of Detroit. From that experience, and in the years since, I've recognized that in the wake of trauma, survivors face a huge and dangerous problem—a harrowing sense of isolation.

You may feel that you are all alone, with an overwhelming sense of both isolation and separation. Trauma can set off a domino effect of psychological regression. By "regression," I mean the temporary loss of emotional and cognitive capacities, skills, and resources.

With trauma from a brain injury, for example, a cascade of metabolic changes result in an alteration in brain chemistry. The changes impact how you feel about yourself, others, and the world. It's as if a tornado has ripped through your life and left you petrified and grief stricken. Your cognitive and behavioral problems can be so severe and persistent that finding proper diagnosis and treatment is critical. If this has been your experience, you are not alone. Know that there are people and processes available to help you heal.

THE POWER OF EMPATHY

Sometimes, empathy and a hug from a caring person can spark a shift back from the depths of despair and hopelessness born of psychological regression. Because the whirlwind pull of these dark forces is powerful, it is sometimes impossible to feel any positivity unless you are open to accepting the helping hands and hearts of other compassionate individuals.

As with many things in life, we must reconcile the fact that we cannot always win battles alone and must accept help. It is a strength, not a personal weakness, to ask for and receive care.

Many people value their sense of independence above all else. Injuries often strip us of that freedom. It's humbling to have to wait for someone to pick you up and drive you to a medical or legal appointment, or have someone assist you in bathing or help you to understand written text. It's normal to feel and to grieve a sense of losing independence. Know that it's okay to receive. Accept empathy from others.

THE ROLE OF PREACCIDENT TRAUMA

When you are in an accident, you bring your history with you. Sometimes this history includes previous traumatic life events that can have a sensitizing effect. These experiences magnify the consequences of the recent collision beyond those expected from a single accident. You may need to work through unresolved prior traumatic events—perhaps an earlier auto crash, previous injuries, or other traumatic life events—before you can draw upon your inner resources to contend with your current auto-injury trauma.

Disturbing emotions connected to preaccident traumatic life events may be evoked. It seems we store traumatic memories differently from regular memories. A new distressing experience can open the storage closet in our minds to many unresolved emotions.

Effects of Preaccident Brain Traumas

We now know that cumulative blows to the head can cause a severe condition known as Cumulative Traumatic Encephalopathy (CTE), often diagnosed in professional athletes. CTE was named by neuropathologist Bennet Omalu when he first identified the deteriorating effects of multiple concussions or subconcussive injuries on the brains of former NFL players.

Many of us have some history of experiencing hits to the head, but those injuries are not in the same league as the multiple concussions that NFL football players or other professional athletes often sustain. Omalu's work and its widespread coverage by journalist Jeanne Marie Laskas in a 2009 *GQ Magazine* article inspired the creation of the movie *Concussion* starring Will Smith as Dr. Omalu. This film helped to heighten public awareness of the effects of brain trauma and society's desire to deny them.

For the average person, a long-forgotten concussion can still have a sensitizing effect on subsequent concussive forces. Unfortunately, the current system of grading a traumatic brain injury as mild, moderate, or severe does not consider the fact that *any* harm to the brain can cause significant disruption of functioning in all areas of life. In fact, we have no accurate way to determine just how severe or debilitating a head injury will be. Every brain is unique and no two brain injuries are the same.

Symptoms like memory loss, confusion, impaired judgment, paranoia, and impulse control problems often appear along with aggression, depression, and eventually, progressive dementia. Sometimes a concussion from an auto accident can be amplified due to a sensitizing or priming effect. When your brain doesn't work as expected, it can feel overwhelming, confusing, and absolutely terrifying. All the positive thinking in the world will be ineffective until the underlying causes of these symptoms can be correctly identified and treated.

Andrew Marr, a former Green Beret, endured multiple TBIs (Traumatic Brain Injuries) as a result of his military deployments. He suffered for years before he connected with California neuroendocrinologist Dr. Mark Gordon, and learned about the physical side of TBI. In his book, *Tales from the Blast Factory*, Marr says, "Trying to navigate life with a brain or body riddled with inflammation and coupled with hormonal deficiencies is comparable to planting flowers in sand. Most plants will not grow or thrive in such an environment. The brain and body are no different."[2]

By understanding that the brain has a remarkable ability to heal and that specific therapies can help, hope and relief can be generated. Often, we must accept the need to make adaptations in response to physical and cognitive loss. This can be difficult.

GRIEF WORK IS IMPORTANT

As my training psychoanalyst Henry Krystal—a Holocaust survivor, psychiatrist, psychoanalyst, and pioneer in traumatic stress—emphasized to me, "Good therapy is good grieving." Psychotherapy often involves doing the deep work of accepting what we have lost through grieving. Undertaking grief work is often essential for survivors of trauma.

Through therapy, survivors also learn that, sometimes, minor changes can be profoundly transformative. Usually, recovering a sense of self helps to reclaim one's life, one small piece at a time. It can be as simple as taking a short walk or calling an old friend or a family member. Mental health professionals who work with accident victims must continuously remind survivors that they need others. Meaning and connection come from being involved with those who care. As you undertake your recovery, I recommend focusing on positive, life-giving relationships with people who show kindness and consideration.

MAGDA'S STORY

If you are currently suffering from PTSD symptoms, please note that you may find some of the following material disturbing.

For Magda, psychotherapy was a lifesaver. Magda was a vibrant 25-year-old who enjoyed motorcycle riding with her husband. One beautiful summer day, a distracted driver lost control of his vehicle. The collision flipped their bike. Magda suffered broken bones and was later diagnosed with a traumatic brain injury. She had problems focusing, persistent headaches, difficulty with her short-term memory, and wildly fluctuating emotions. She also suffered a painful road rash over large areas of her body. When the skin didn't heal, she required several surgeries and skin grafts. The grafts became infected, which meant further emotional turmoil and hospitalization.

Magda quickly discovered that she needed help with the sometimes frightening and confusing emotions she was experiencing. She had violent mood swings, and at times, her anger became volatile. Dealing with her spouse, who struggled with his own injuries, added further challenges to her recovery. She began to feel that finding her way through this experience on her own was nearly impossible.

When she entered weekly individual and group therapy, she relaxed and found new strength and direction. She had been through other traumatic events in her life, but this accident was the first time she'd ever questioned her sanity. By learning that she was not alone and that her experiences were normal for her condition, she began her journey toward emotional healing. Today, she has returned to work and is considering going back to graduate studies in social work.

CINDY'S STORY

Cindy finds that being positive is the key to healing. If she lets herself spiral down and hit rock bottom, she fears she might not get up again.

She typically gets only two to three hours of sleep a night due to unrelenting pain in her leg, head, and back. Most nights, when she does drift off, she experiences intense, vivid, and horrifying nightmares involving gruesome images of injury and threats of death.

She shared with me how the trauma to her brain has affected her and how difficult it is for her family and friends to understand her new limitations and peculiarities of speech and memory. In psychotherapy sessions, we spoke not only about how the psychological defense mechanism of denial makes it hard for family members to come to grips with the injury but also how denial operates to protect one's self from confronting the effects of a pervasive and daunting brain injury along with other traumas to the body.

"You know you have it," Cindy said, "but you deny that something's wrong. When you realize that you've put the TV remote in your fridge, it's not a good thing! Or when you call your son by the dog's name, you know you said something wrong, but your brain doesn't register that as quickly as you'd want it to."

Cindy relates having to use step-by-step thoughts to get through everyday tasks such as doing the dishes or dusting the furniture. "Before the accident, it was so easy. I didn't have to think. I just did it. My brain worked automatically. Now, when the phone rings, I have to think, 'Oh, the phone's ringing. I think I need to pick it up.'"

Cindy's world has totally shifted. Does she feel like a different person? Yes. At first, she wasn't okay with that. But as she noticed herself doing things differently and accepted that she was no longer the person she had been, she became more positive: "You have to fall in love with who you've become so you can function as a normal person.

"You have to find a little light at the end of the dark tunnel," she says, "and grab it with every power you have—all your strength—to catch the little light and pull it back to you, because otherwise you're lost."

FINDING NEW LIFE MEANING

Because people are complex, it is essential to address some of the fundamental intricacies of being human. From years of clinical work, I've realized that Viktor Frankl, an Austrian neurologist and psychiatrist imprisoned in the Nazi camps, was correct in his point that our need to search for and find meaning in our lives is key to our mental health.[3] Just as Frankl discovered this essential need in the despair of Nazi Germany death camps, many car-accident survivors also come to the same realization on their long roads to recovery.

Psychotherapist Eric Maisel reminds us that a core component of mental health is doing what makes us feel pride. He sees this practice as even more important than a search for meaning. Pursuing a feeling of pride is a useful conceptual tool in trauma recovery.

Psychotherapy is about finding meaning. In therapy, we work to make psychological sense of events, feelings, thoughts, relationships, and dreams. Making sense of the meaning of traumatic events is the focus of therapy with accident victims. Survivors are often plagued by "what if" thinking after an accident. "If I hadn't forgotten my coffee, and if I hadn't gone back in the house to get it, I wouldn't have been at the intersection when I was hit."

From years of working with patients to help them come to terms with traumatic events, I've come to appreciate the importance of acknowledging fate. Even stronger than fate is the belief that things happen according to a larger, mysterious plan.

Many survivors come to feel that their car accident was actually a blessing in disguise as it led them on a path to an even greater, more fulfilling life trajectory, a higher life purpose, and a more profound sense of who they are. They often feel a deeper appreciation for the complexities of relationships and the vital need for human connectedness and love.

When you begin your recovery process, it is challenging to comprehend ever feeling optimistic about your future, but it is essential to keep faith and keep going. Learn to adopt a positive attitude and accept your circumstances; encouraging changes will occur.

The richness of life comes from the experience and appreciation of contrasts. Psychotherapy can empower us to recognize these contrasts so we can choose that which we want, be it war or peace, connectedness or isolation, inner peace or worry, illness or health.

There may be anxiety-provoking uncertainties to confront. Will surgery make me better or worse? Will the pain medication give me relief and make me more functional or create addiction and more significant health problems? Will returning to work now make me stronger or injure me further?

Remember that information is powerful. Answers to the above questions require gathering the right information. Ask questions and collect evidence from trusted sources. The Pete Seeger song, "Turn, Turn, Turn," is an apt metaphor for the postaccident trauma experience and the turns we must take in life once we are injured or compromised. Your goal is to reclaim your life by creating an even more fulfilling existence.

TIPS

- *Know that recovery doesn't happen overnight. Take it one day at a time.*
- *Take control of managing your pain.*
- *Be kind and patient with yourself.*

2

COMMON CONDITIONS

Many individuals and accident victims do not realize that the chemicals in the body mask many pain and severe injury symptoms. This is a direct response to the trauma you suffered in the crash. Therefore, it is common that a few days or even weeks later, your pain symptoms will begin to appear and grow increasingly worse if left untreated.

—Dr. Harry W. Brown[1]

Auto accidents can destroy your body, your mind, your family, and the life you have always known, in a flash. Each story presented in this book contains elements of potentially devastating auto-accident effects. As you read, remember the following: You are not alone in your experience nor in your journey to your "new normal," be it temporary or permanent. Do not think of yourself as in better or worse shape than the people you will meet in these pages; instead, see the common ground you share. Consider the hope, understanding, and peace their stories can bring to your life. While you may not imagine it now, you may one day see the blessings bestowed by the tremendous trials standing before you today.

The journey for those badly injured in a car wreck should start in the emergency room of a trauma hospital. (Note: My advice is to immediately get to the best hospital emergency department you can find. You are likely in shock and not in a position to self-evaluate your health status.) The first treatment priority is to save your life. From there, assessment and treatment moves to diagnostic imaging studies, cleaning and repairing lacerations, reducing and setting fractures, applying braces to sprained joints, or full-on surgery for internal injuries. However, the initial hospital treatment is only the beginning. Diagnosing the extent of your injuries can be an ongoing process. Recovery often takes much, much longer than you might expect.

TREATED AND RELEASED

An area that urgently needs to be addressed is the emergency department care of auto-crash survivors. Susan received emergency treatment at a premier university hospital after a severe auto crash that took one person's life. After three days in the hospital with no one addressing her severe post-traumatic symptoms of flashbacks, panic, and nightmares, she was released with a clean bill of health. Two months after her hospital discharge, she was diagnosed with PTSD, a moderate TBI (traumatic brain injury), and fractured spinal vertebra.

Unfortunately, this is not an uncommon story. Hospital emergency departments need to do better in their evaluation and treatment of auto-crash survivors. Three years ago, I participated in a McGraw-Hill podcast, directed at medical students, which addressed these issues. The need for a massive overhaul of the emergency department care of auto-crash survivors is a necessity. Perhaps, with education, we can make a change.

Here are suggestions regarding your initial hospital treatment:

1. Tell the healthcare providers *everything* about your symptoms and injuries.
2. Try to make sure they document all that you report.

3. Be sure you know everything you have been diagnosed with. Take notes or have relatives or friends, who were not in the accident, take notes for you.

Once you leave the hospital, do not drive until you know you are safe to be on the road. I have seen people with undiagnosed brain injuries given their car keys at the hospital with no concerns about the driver's potential safety. Dangers related to a postconcussive mental status often involve extreme anxiety and confusion. Some injuries to the brain result in a lack of awareness of a disability or condition. This inability to recognize a deficit in self-awareness is termed *anosognosia*. Anosognosia can prevent a patient from getting the help needed to move forward in their recovery.

It is advisable to receive an evaluation from a driver-rehabilitation specialist trained in brain injury or severe anxiety before driving again. These specialists are typically occupational therapists trained in assessing and assisting a driver's post-injury ability to drive safely. Many of my patients who sustained brain injuries say they should have had this evaluation before driving again. They found themselves getting into difficulties on the road due to concentration problems, impaired attention, confusion, and anxiety.

Due to the physical mechanics of car accidents and the g-forces brought to bear on the human body, many injuries do not surface until weeks, months, or even years after the collision. On your journey to recovery, you may go through the frustrating experience of working with numerous healthcare professionals before you discover the right team. Your practitioners should reach the correct diagnosis and create a treatment plan specific to you. It is vital to your healing that you find informed professionals who can provide competent, caring service and guide you through the complex difficulties involved in your recovery. You will then be empowered to take charge of your recovery and to form healthy, collaborative relationships with members of your professional healthcare team.

THE PHYSICAL SIDE OF INJURY

What are the most common accident-related conditions? Lacerations, broken bones, whiplash, strained or sprained muscles, and, in the most devastating cases, brain injury, spinal injury, paralysis, or death.

Marilyn, mentioned in chapter 1, did not have visible physical injuries. She'd been bounced around in her vehicle after being T-boned by a driver on their cell phone. Marilyn refused to acknowledge anything was wrong. She wanted to get back to her busy life working and tending to her family. It was months before the extent of her pain and physical injuries were finally diagnosed and treated.

If you are currently suffering from PTSD symptoms, please note that you may find some of the following material disturbing.

Jason, another patient, was so physically broken after his motorcycle was hit by two vehicles that a complete description of his injuries would fill several pages. Motorcycle versus car rarely ends well for the motorcyclist. Here's the short version: In the collision, Jason flew through the air, bounced across the pavement, and landed with pieces of his bike on top of him. His severed foot lay next to his head. His jaw was split down the center, and most of his molars were sheared off. He had a ruptured eardrum and four skull fractures, and his tailbone had detached from some of the surrounding muscles. Not only was his right collarbone cracked, but many of his ribs were also broken. He also incurred severe road rash over parts of his body, and bones in his spine were damaged.

For you, Marilyn, Jason, and the other survivors you will soon meet throughout these pages, the day of the collision marks the start of a new existence. Phase One is a state of shock and confusion. You know neither the extent of your injuries nor what to do about them. Phase Two is spent learning about your health challenges and putting together a professional team to facilitate your recovery. Phase Three—often the most prolonged phase—is the act of measuring your healing progress and the movement toward new opportunities in life. Embrace your "new normal" and see yourself as a survivor who has not only successfully grieved the loss of your pre-injury self, but who is also flourishing. In Phase Three, you'll begin to adopt a resilient self-identity that can embrace post-traumatic growth.

Whiplash

According to the American Chiropractic Association, approximately two-thirds of people involved in motor vehicle accidents develop symptoms of whiplash.[2] When the head suddenly and forcefully moves backward and then forward, the neck can be deeply impacted. Auto-accident survivors are frequently given a diagnosis of whiplash in the hospital emergency room. The term "whiplash" is used because the injury occurs after the harsh whipping of the neck and the head during an accident. According to the Mayo Clinic, this violent motion can injure bones in the spine, ligaments, muscles, nerves, and other tissues of the neck.[3]

The primary whiplash symptoms are pain in the neck and shoulders, headaches, and stiffness. Dizziness, fatigue, and numbness in the arms, sleep disturbance, problems with memory and concentration, irritability, blurred vision, tinnitus, and depression can also occur. The mechanism of a whiplash injury can also be a cause of damage to the brain, and a TBI shares many of the same symptoms.

Whiplash injuries are common in rear-end-type accidents due to the mechanical forces on the body. Most victims improve within weeks, but in severe cases, chronic pain and other complications can result.

Headaches related to this injury typically start at the base of the skull. It is common to have a related condition termed *cervicocranial pain syndrome* or *craniocervical junction disorder*. MRI or CT imaging studies can help to confirm a diagnosis.

Chiropractic or Osteopathic Manipulative Treatment (OMT) is often helpful for treating whiplash injuries. Sometimes, significant relief from related headache pain can be achieved from these noninvasive treatments. It is essential to confirm, via MRIs, that it's safe to do these manipulations.

Traumatic Brain Injury (TBI)

A TBI can result from a sudden, violent hit or hits to the head. For example, banging the dashboard, window, or headrest in a car accident; being slammed with a baseball bat; an explosive blast such as experienced by miners and soldiers; a sharp object piercing the skull and entering the brain tissue; falling off a bike; and so on. Because most TBIs are noninvasive, they are often overlooked or misdiagnosed. We will take an extensive look at TBIs in chapter 4.

Postconcussion Syndrome (PCS)

PCS is a mild form of traumatic brain injury (TBI). Immediate symptoms include headache and dizziness. Later symptoms—sometimes occurring days or weeks after impact—include noise and light sensitivity, problems with concentration and memory, fatigue, irritability, depression, anxiety, and loss of interest and motivation. PCS symptoms generally resolve over several weeks to a year.

Cognitive Disorders (CDs)

CDs are acquired mental conditions that affect abilities such as learning, memory, perception, reasoning, judgment, and problem solving. CDs can result from a traumatic brain injury and inflammation in the brain, as well as depression and anxiety that often stem from the complex interplay of physical and psychological trauma.

Tinnitus

One of the most common and distressing problems serious car-accident survivors encounter is tinnitus (ringing in the ear). With tinnitus, there is no external source of the sound, yet a ringing or buzzing plays continuously or intermittently in your head. It can be caused by injury to the brain, inner ear, or even the jaw. My dentist friend, Dr. Richard Klein, a TMD (temporomandibular disorder) specialist, says that some forms of tinnitus can result from muscular injuries and misalignments of the jaw that impact structures of the inner ear. Not only can tinnitus lead to deep depression with suicidal thinking, but it can also cause a major disruption to one's life. Much research is underway to find effective treatments. Often tinnitus accompanies symptoms of dizziness, vertigo, or problems with balance. It is essential to be evaluated by an audiologist, as well as ENT (ear, nose, and throat) and TMD specialists to pinpoint causes.

Airbags—Friends or Foe?[4]

How effective are seat belts and airbags at preventing traumatic brain injuries? A research study by Frank A. Pintar, Narayan Yoganandan, and Thomas Gennarelli examined the U.S. DOT NASS database files from 1991 to 1998, evaluating drivers and right–front seat occupants in frontal crashes.[5] They found that head injuries occur in 2.76 percent of those restrained by seat belt alone and 3.51 percent by those in which both airbag and belt systems were employed. Unrestrained drivers had a 10.39 percent incidence of at least one type of head injury.[6] These numbers are meager compared to what we have learned about diagnosing brain injuries since 1991.

Although designed to prevent loss of life, airbag deployment is not 100 percent effective and can cause traumatic brain injuries and, surprisingly, death.[7] Also, the noise levels associated with the shotgun-level blast of an airbag deploying can lead to permanent hearing loss and tinnitus. Studies show that the peak acoustic pressure of 170 dB (range 150–170 dB) can cause damaging inner ear effects.[8] Other writers indicate that it is rare for sensorineural hearing loss to occur from airbag deployment, although many of my patients suffer from tinnitus, dizziness, and vertigo in association with brain injuries, particularly after surviving high-impact crashes that involve airbag deployment.[9]

Cerebral Spinal Fluid (CSF) Leaks

I only recently learned about this condition when hearing about a suspected trauma related to a CSF (cerebral spinal fluid) leak. My patient complained of persistent drainage of a clear fluid from one nostril from the time of her auto crash more than a year ago. Medical investigations are currently underway due to persistent self-advocacy to find out if this is indeed a CSF leak.

Writing about this is crucial because it appears this condition is frequently missed and there are effective treatments that in many cases can dramatically eliminate or reduce the associated symptoms that can greatly diminish functioning and quality of life.

One of the injuries that can result from trauma to the head, including injury due to rotational forces, involves tearing of the outer protective layer of the brain. This layer is called the dura mater or sometimes just dura. The Latin term translates as "tough or hard matter." Once a tear or hole develops in the dura, CSF can leak out just as a hole in a plumbing pipe would allow water to leak out. CSF is a clear, colorless fluid that circulates in the brain and spinal cord. The fluid acts as protection and functions to deliver nutrients and remove waste. CSF contains a unique protein called Beta-2-transferrin that is produced in the brain. When Beta-2 is detected in the fluid, it confirms that there is leakage of CSF leading to a diagnosis of the condition. Testing for Beta-2-transferrin is done by a method called *immune-fixation electrophoresis*.[10]

The most common of all symptoms related to a CSF leak are persistent headaches. According to the Cleveland Clinic, CFS leaks are commonly misdiagnosed as migraines, other headaches, or sinusitis.[11] Characteristic symptoms include many of those we frequently see in car-crash survivors: headaches, vision changes, hearing changes, sensitivity to sound, sensitivity to light, balance problems, neck stiffness and neck pain, nausea or vomiting, pain between the shoulder blades, and arm pain.

The Cleveland Clinic indicates that other symptoms unique to CSF leaks in the skull include the following: clear watery drainage usually from only one side of the nose or one ear when tilting the head forward, salty or metallic taste in the mouth, drainage down the back of the throat, and loss of smell.

Several medical tests can be performed to investigate possible CSF leaks: computed tomography (CT), magnetic resonance imaging (MRI), myelography, cisternography, and lumbar puncture. Treatments range from the conservative, such as bed rest and hydration, to the invasive, including surgery. The required treatment will depend on the cause and location of the leak.

Ian Carroll, MD, is a pain specialist who helped develop Stanford's Neuroradiology and Neurology Headache Division's CSF Leak Headache Program, after his daughter suffered an initially undiagnosed CSF leak. Dr. Carroll indicated that nausea and vomiting can be the main symptoms of a CSF leak. Also, since CSF is connected to inner ear fluid, changes in pressure of the CSF due to leakage can cause the pressure in the inner ear to change, which can result in tinnitus. Problems with concentration, fatigue, task persistence, and neck pain can be concurrent symptoms, as well as other uncommon, nondescript neurological symptoms.

Dr. Carroll also stated that CSF leaks are commonly missed in hospital emergency departments. Whiplash injuries are one of the four leading causes of CSF leaks. He cited a research study in Japan conducted by S. Ishikawa and others that examined 66 patients with chronic whiplash-associated symptoms, including complaints of neck and head pain and difficulty with fatigue or memory.[12] Imaging studies with radionuclide cisternogram revealed 37 of them were positive for a CSF leak. After receiving treatment, about half of the patients with a CSF leak who were disabled were able to return to work.

According to the Spinal CSF Leak Foundation, there are several symptoms associated with the condition, the most common being an "upright" or positional headache.[13] This type of headache gets worse after sitting up and intensifies as the day goes on. The CSF leak can often be repaired medically (but not always) and will sometimes repair itself. In addition to the symptoms listed above, other symptoms often include brain fog, being off-balance, and tremor.

The Spinal CSF Leak Foundation states that many physicians are not familiar with CSF leaks. There are lists with many helpful resources for providers and patients on their website, which is listed in the Resources section at the back of this book.

Auto-crash injuries can require much time and effort to untangle. Future research into and diagnostics for whiplash injuries that present with the symptoms we commonly see should consider and rule out CSF leaks.

THE PSYCHOLOGICAL SIDE OF INJURY

While physical healing can take a long time—years, or even decades—sometimes getting beyond the impact of the crash is made even more challenging by the effects of psychological injuries. Many mental health issues go unnoticed or undiagnosed, which makes the overall journey to wellness seem endless—even futile. Obtaining a quick, accurate diagnosis of all of your conditions is not only crucial to your healing but also is a vital factor when dealing with the legal and insurance side of your circumstances. The longer it takes to determine your postaccident conditions—physical and psychological—the more difficult the insurance and legal matters will become.

Dealing with the legal and insurance ramifications of your injury can be a huge source of stress, and metaphorical headaches, that few people anticipate. Most of us do not understand the importance of knowing what is covered by our auto insurance. If you don't know, believe me, you will quickly find out *after* an accident.

When viewed as connected with the physical healing process, common psychological injuries become easier to diagnose and treat. Before listing examples, I want to remind you of the connection between our bodies and minds. What happens in one always affects the other. Fortunately, promising new work and treatments by neuroendocrinologists address how common trauma-related psychological conditions often stem from hormonal imbalances that result from physical trauma. More detail will be discussed in chapter 4, which deals with traumatic brain injury.

Post-Traumatic Stress Disorder

Most people who've experienced or witnessed a terrifying event display symptoms of PTSD despite not meeting full diagnostic criteria. Mounting evidence suggests that the symptoms indicate that an injured brain does not fully process distressing human experiences. Post-traumatic stress disorder can be delayed and not manifest until well after an accident. Symptoms may include strong and unwanted memories of the event, nightmares, emotional numbness, flashbacks, anxiety, intense guilt or worry, angry outbursts, feeling "on edge," and avoiding thoughts and situations that are reminders of the trauma, and they may not show up for days, weeks, months, or even years later.[14]

PTSD can be disabling and can expand into more generalized anxiety and depressive conditions that can severely restrict daily functioning and quality of life. With the proper treatment and support, the prognosis is good.

Many people have preexisting, unresolved trauma that reactivates after an auto accident. Past issues must be resolved before the current ones can be remedied. As an example, a survivor's loved one died in a car accident years before, but the emotional impact had never been addressed. A combination of two or more traumatic events that create psychological symptoms can cause Complex PTSD. This condition is more challenging to treat and can slow progress. Chapter 3 details the many "faces" of PTSD.

Anxiety and Panic Disorders

Anxiety—including worry, nervousness, and/or unease—is fear wrapped in distressing thoughts and apprehensions based on "what ifs." An event or an uncertain outcome can unexpectedly bring on anxiety. Panic disorders are similar but distinct in that the anxiety and fear appear abruptly with more intense physical symptoms such as chest pains, difficulty breathing, rapid heart rate, and sweating. Panic attacks can be set off by events that remind you of your accident or by triggers outside of your awareness. They can be

severely distressing and immobilizing. Due to the physical symptoms of panic attacks, it is essential to rule out a possible physiological cause, such as a heart condition.

Depression

I cannot think of a single car-accident survivor who has not experienced considerable depression resulting from pain, disability issues,
and lowered quality of life. Often far-reaching and immobilizing,
depression is graded as mild, moderate, or severe. Depression is
magnified when isolation and withdrawal from others is a factor. In
graduate school, we were taught that depression is the opposite of
expression. "De-" versus "Ex-." Thoughts, feelings, and concerns
need to be released and verbally expressed.

Often, suicidal thinking can be an expression of depression. If
you are having suicidal thoughts, please do not keep them to yourself. There are people who care and who can help. Find a supportive
person to talk to and share with. There is also free support available
by phone and online through suicide prevention organizations. If
you are in immediate danger of harming yourselves or others, please
call your country's emergency number (911 in the United States) or
get to your nearest hospital emergency department.

Anger and Frustration

It is common to experience high levels of frustration and anger
following an accident. Many stressors you will encounter will lead
to heightened emotions. This can manifest as anger toward others,
which in turn creates feelings of guilt. The feelings of guilt fuel
more depression and anxiety. Some, who continue to drive, experience road rage combined with anxiety and fears about getting into
another accident. If you were the cause of the crash, there are additional layers of emotion to work through and come to peace with.
You must own responsibility, learn from your error, and do the
psychological work necessary to ensure you don't repeat it.

Know that the complexity of physical and emotional recovery is great and calls for much self-advocacy with your medical providers to get to the root of persistent symptoms. As you journey through your process of recovery, it is crucial to delve further into symptoms that are not responding to a mainline approach of diagnosis, medications, and procedures.

TIPS

- *Find a team of informed healthcare professionals.*
- *Get full medical versus coordinated benefits on your auto insurance policy if you can. For severe injuries, the costs of care can run into the millions. Full medical coverage will help to ensure that you receive all the coverage you require.*
- *There are a variety of homeopathic remedies that many of my patients find useful for panic attacks. Find an experienced homeopath who can make recommendations.*

3

WHAT IS POST-TRAUMATIC STRESS?

PTSD: It's not the person refusing to let go of the past, but the past refusing to let go of the person.

—Unknown

Unlike other forms of psychological disorders, the core issue in trauma is reality.

—Bessel A. van der Kolk[1]

SOMETHING CRAZY HAPPENED TO YOU

Nearly eight million American adults each year suffer from post-traumatic stress disorder (PTSD), which can also develop in children. From my clinical experience treating hundreds of survivors, I know that auto accidents are a significant cause of PTSD. In my practice, most survivors experience the disorder to some degree. While you or your family and friends may know something is wrong, you may not consider that what you are experiencing is PTSD. Your first encounters with symptoms such as flashbacks, irritability, and avoidance can cause you or those close to you to think you are going crazy.

The first step to finding the right treatment is to recognize the signs of PTSD and acknowledge these experiences as normal reactions to an abnormal event. It is gratifying to see the visible relief patients have when told their symptoms are normal in relation to the traumatic event they experienced, and that no, they are *not* crazy. Rather, something crazy has happened *to* them. It's a relief when patients realize the symptoms can be lessened and resolved.

THE HISTORY OF PTSD

For as long as humans have inhabited the planet, stressors have had long-term effects on behavior. Adverse experiences have always been a part of life. Our ancestors likely had the same psychological reaction to an attack by a saber-toothed tiger as we have to an act of terrorism, a bomb blast, or a car crash. As a result of walking past a construction site where jackhammers cause the cement to vibrate, survivors of earthquakes might experience flashbacks to that horrid day.

Our first task in healing from a traumatic event is to regain a sense of safety, and this can be challenging. We often need caring support to reach this crucial objective. Sadly, some of us have had little experience of safety in our lives, and experiencing a feeling of safety through therapy takes time.

Lessons from War

According to the U.S. Department of Veterans Affairs, Austrian physician Josef Leopold wrote in 1796 of soldiers who experienced anxiety and trouble sleeping as a result of military trauma.

At the end of World War I, what we now label as PTSD was called "shell shock" or "war neuroses" because symptoms would appear after exposure to exploding artillery shells.[2] We now know that explosions can cause concussive waves of energy, known as blast waves, which pass through the body and can cause injury as well as disrupt brain functioning.

In 1980, PTSD was first officially introduced as a diagnosis in the American Psychiatric Association's *DSM* (*Diagnostic and Statistical Manual of Mental Disorders*) and was conceptualized as an anxiety disorder that developed after seeing or living through an event that caused severe harm or death. The diagnosis was derived from Vietnam veterans and a group of mental health professionals who attempted to recognize symptoms and help the soldiers cope with the psychological aftermath of the war. Common indicators became codified into what has become our current definition of PTSD.

The American Psychiatric Association's acceptance of PTSD as a diagnosis was a pivotal step. For the first time, PTSD was considered a result of outside stressors rather than inherent individual weakness.[3]

A diagnosis of PTSD was initially applied strictly to combat soldiers who were "shocked" by and unable to face their experiences of combat. At first, the diagnosis was not accepted by many mental health professionals or by the general public; however, over the past four decades, American society and the majority of mental health professionals have embraced it. The disorder has also expanded to apply to any traumatic event and serious loss that evokes strong emotions of terror, loss, and grief.

The Evolution of PTSD

The Evil Hours: *A Biography of Post-Traumatic Stress Disorder* is one of the best books I have read on PTSD.[4] The author, David J. Morris, is not a mental health clinician but a former Marine infantry officer who worked as a reporter in Iraq from 2004 to 2007. He wrote his book after he received an award that offered a creative writing fellowship from the National Endowment for the Arts. Morris began his study of PTSD after he was almost killed in a Humvee hit by roadside bomb explosion in Baghdad. He writes about the history of psychological trauma and researched as far back as the Greek work of Homer, *The Iliad*, written nearly three thousand years ago. Homer described at least two symptoms of PTSD suffered by the iconic warrior Achilles.

Morris cites the work of literary historian Paul Fussell who studied the clay tablets from four thousand years ago that detail the aftermath of a great battle in the land of Sumer (now known as Iraq). In those tablets, known as the *Lamentation of Ur*, the writer describes his symptom—considered the hallmark of PTSD—sleep disturbance. The ancient insomniac wrote, "The storm's cyclone like destruction—verily its terror has filled me full. Because of its affliction in my nightly sleeping place, I have no peace."[5]

Since the introduction of the clinical diagnosis of PTSD, the details and specifics have gone through several modifications with subsequent editions of the *DSM*. In the current version of the *DSM-5*, PTSD is placed under the category of Trauma- and Stressor-Related Disorders. The *DSM-5* code is 309.81, but mental health professionals now use F43.10 from the International Classification for Diseases (ICD-10-CM), which has become the required source.

In the *DSM-5*, symptom criteria from five categories must be met to officially qualify as full-on PTSD. In clinical reality, if you don't fully meet the current diagnostic criteria, you can still be considered to have a trauma-related disorder that dramatically diminishes your quality of life and severely compromises your functionality. Some research studies are misleading because they report PTSD as being resolved by some treatment that knocked out a criterion that had pushed a subject over the line into the official diagnosis. In actuality, the subject's quality of life was still poor from the lingering effects of trauma.

Because PTSD was initially tied to war trauma and is, in many ways, "owned" by the Department of Veterans Affairs, other forms of civilian trauma have taken rear seats on the PTSD trauma bus. Car crashes are the number one cause of PTSD, yet the International Society for Traumatic Stress Studies, ruled mainly by academics closely associated with the VA, pay little attention to car-accident trauma. This is why I propose the term Vehicular Trauma Syndrome to more closely align with the trauma-related symptoms these survivors manifest.

While first conceptualized as a psychological reaction to extreme events, PTSD is now considered a psychobiological mental disorder that results in changes in brain function and structure. This awareness becomes essential when we consider that PTSD has, on some occasions, been used by government agencies to minimize the body side of the mind-body connection in order to avoid paying service-related benefits. Recognition of this mind-body relationship is vital to recovery.

One particular feature of PTSD, which makes it unique, is that the manifestation of symptoms can be delayed—with only subtle signs appearing initially and severe symptoms appearing months, or in some cases even years, post-event.

While most people experience only a transient, distressing psychological reaction to trauma exposure (an acute stress reaction), a smaller group develops chronic symptoms that can severely impair functioning. Many factors have been studied and proposed as predictive of who will develop PTSD, including prior exposure to trauma.

Since its introduction, PTSD has been heavily researched by scientists. Brain structures playing critical roles in PTSD include the amygdala, hippocampus, anterior cingulate, insula, and orbitofrontal region.

Modern brain research demonstrates changes in brain structures in patients with PTSD; however, causation is problematic. The hippocampus, a seahorse-shaped structure deep within our brains involved in regulating emotion, motivation, learning, and memory, has been shown to have a reduced volume in both PTSD and TBI patients. In cases of fibromyalgia, the hippocampus is often dysregulated. Some pathological features of PTSD overlap with features found in patients who have suffered traumatic brain injuries.[6] The overlap in the pathophysiology of PTSD and TBI will be diligently studied over the coming years. I believe that the role of hormones and the endocrine system will be central in this research, particularly involving the stress hormones and their interactions with the endocrine system.

The good news is that the changes to the hippocampus and other structures seen in PTSD patients *can be reversed* under specific conditions, which include therapy, medication, and exercise. The ability of the brain to change is called *neuroplasticity.* We now believe the brain can "rewire" neuronal connections around damaged areas to restore vital functions.

Many forms of treatment for PTSD symptoms have been studied and are currently utilized. Talk therapy, cognitive-behavioral therapy, EMDR, tapping therapy, medications, exposure therapy, and hallucinogens are several of the most common.

EXAMPLES FROM VEHICULAR TRAUMA INCIDENTS

Flashbacks and Recurrent Nightmares

Fifty-three-year-old Sandy was rear-ended in 2015. She sustained a forceful neck injury (whiplash), a TBI, and injuries to her lower back and right shoulder, which eventually required surgical repair.

"I had the same or similar nightmares in the beginning," she says. "I was running, and a big steamroller rolled on top of me. I could hear everything in my body crunching and squirting. It was impossible to get back to sleep after that."

Dreaming is thought to take place during a phase of sleep called Rapid Eye Movement (REM). Some research suggests that people coping with trauma enter the REM phase much faster than average and are quickly subjected to distressing dream content. When you know you will face terror and horror if you go to sleep, you may avoid closing your eyes.

Avoidance and Withdrawal

Janet remembers that she and a friend were on their way to church, but she has no memory of the crash that left them both stuffed underneath a semitrailer truck nor of the emergency personnel using the Jaws of Life to get them out. That was four years ago, and she still has panic attacks when she comes close to semitrailer trucks on the road.

"I can't breathe. Sometimes I start screaming. It takes me a long time to calm down. People hate driving me places; I'm a nervous wreck by the time we get to our destination."

Because her reactions are so strong, Janet avoids going anywhere that involves getting into a car. "I used to be very outgoing. Any time I was invited to something, I was the first one there. I was a social butterfly. Now, most of the time, I just say, 'No,' so I don't ruin everyone's evening because I'm having a bad day."

Memory Problems and Feelings of Detachment

One early French psychologist who studied traumatic memory and dissociation was Pierre Janet (1859–1947). He wrote about disorders of remembrance (*troubles du souvenir*) and referred to what he observed as either too much (intrusions) or too little (dissociation) remembering of the trauma.

The memory issue in PTSD for auto-crash survivors is problematic because there is also often an issue of brain trauma. Working through the accident trauma is like looking at a smashed, broken, glass plate, attempting to put the pieces back in place and viewing it again from many different angles. There are often painful emotions attached to each shard of experience.

During this process of therapeutic review, repressed memories are frequently retrieved and used to help the survivor accept, on an emotional level, what has happened. Often looking at photographs of the damaged car can jog memories that culminate in trauma resolution. (It is particularly challenging when a survivor has no memory of the accident due to being rendered unconscious from a concussion. Driving along one minute, and regaining consciousness in a hospital emergency room the next, can be extremely unnerving and may leave many haunting, unanswered questions.)

I always ask patients for any crash-related photographs so that I can make sense of what they endured. For insurance and legal purposes, photos are also helpful. However, you cannot predict the extent of the physical injuries by how damaged a vehicle appears in a photograph. No two accidents are the same, as the physics and energy dynamics are unique for each.

Steve recalled to me the crunching sound when his car was T-boned in an intersection and he again felt the jolt in his body. He did not just remember the sound, he heard and felt it. An intrusion temporarily hijacks your mind and throws you back into the distressing event that causes you to detach from the here and now. Intrusive memories can be extremely disruptive.

Guilt and Shame

Traumatic experiences, like grief, are often fertile soil for feelings of guilt and shame. A common mind trick we like to play goes something like this: if I am to blame for the trauma, then I have control and need not experience the fear that goes along with a loss of control.

"If only I had left for work on time, the accident would not have happened." This crystal ball gazing is unproductive. You must stop doing it now. Until we can accurately predict future events—down to traffic flow at a particular intersection at an exact future time—you must face the uncomfortable feeling that circumstances beyond our control can have devastating consequences in our lives.

Bethany's life changed on an ordinary day in 2013 when a young woman, so engaged in a phone conversation that she blew through a stop sign at 45 miles per hour, T-boned her.

"Have I lost my mind?" Bethany asks. "I feel totally restricted, and the pain makes me do crazy things. I feel ashamed I cannot be there for my children and husband the way they need me to be.

Some days, I can hardly get myself out of bed and cannot take care of myself, let alone the kids."

LADY GAGA'S PTSD: THE MIND-BODY CONNECTION

In 2016, Lady Gaga made a public announcement about suffering from PTSD and chronic pain as the result of having been sexually assaulted when she was 19 years old. In 2018, she gave several interviews about her experience.[7] Her song, "Til It Happens to You" was written for the documentary *The Hunting Ground*, about the high incidence of sexual assaults on college women and the further trauma they experience as they fight for justice.

It took great courage for Lady Gaga to reveal her personal struggles with PTSD and other health-related issues. She talked about how therapy helped her gain deep insights into ways the trauma had affected her mind, body, and life.

What is most relevant for car-accident survivors is what she shared about her experience of dealing with chronic pain. She spoke of the remaining trauma in the tissues of her body expressing as chronic pain.

Many auto-accident patients experience chronic pain—and not just from sites of fractured bones and vertebrae. The pain they report sometimes has physical correlations that can be seen on imaging studies such as MRIs or CT scans—things like bulging or herniated discs or vertebral fractures. However, some imaging studies are negative, showing no physical trauma or injury, yet the pain symptoms are just as real. While in other cases, the images are positive for bodily injury, yet no pain is associated with the damaged area.

The pain that Lady Gaga experienced is a physical or somatic representation of her trauma—a combination of physical and emotional factors. Our bodies have ways of building monuments to trauma, perhaps as a way of honoring our wounds. For car-accident survivors, pain frequently moves throughout the body in surprising ways.

Several forms of psychotherapy have been developed to address how trauma is stored on a physical level. There is an entire academic field in mental health called *psychosomatic medicine*. One of the newer forms of body-centered psychotherapy is Sensorimotor Psychotherapy developed by Pat Ogden and based on the Hakomi Method (mindfulness, somatic, and experience-based approach to change) of Ron Kurtz.[8] Another is Somatic Experiencing developed by Peter Levine.

One other body-centered psychotherapy, EMDR (Eye Movement Desensitization and Reprocessing), was developed by Francine Shapiro. When Shapiro trained me in EMDR, she confessed that if she had the opportunity to rename her approach, she would simply call it Rapid Processing. EMDR is a powerful tool that incorporates awareness of physical sensation as well as mental images and thoughts. Part of the procedure involves tracking sensations in the body designed to release trauma.

A core idea that runs through these theories is that sensation is the language of the body. It is fascinating to work with a verbal trauma story and then drop into the sensory level of awareness connected to the event(s). Invite your body to tell its story via listening to the sensations it generates. You will be amazed by an entirely new form of conversation that can support trauma release and resolution.

I talk with patients about how the energy that trauma creates can get trapped in the mind and body, which then takes on a life of its own. This energy can produce symptoms and cause debilitating conditions until it can be processed, released, and resolved. We in the trauma field have a saying: *Either you process the trauma, or the trauma will process you.* Often, unprocessed trauma results in substance abuse as a way of self-medicating intense emotions into numbness.

Part of the challenge is for you to overcome the anxieties and fears associated with what has happened. Remember to go slowly, and work with a trusted therapist who can help prevent you from becoming overwhelmed and flooded with emotions that threaten to destabilize you. You can maximize the benefit of trauma work by doing one piece at a time within the safe structure of psychotherapy that's supportive and collaborative.

The severity of your PTSD symptoms can be rated by various psychological tests or inventories that have been developed and researched. When you see a psychologist for a postaccident evaluation, you will be asked to indicate which symptoms you have, along with their frequency and severity. These measures are also a way of tracking progress in your therapy with respect to the frequency and intensity of your symptoms.

TIPS

- *Spend time with positive people.*
- *To reduce a sense of helplessness, volunteer to help others and make a difference.*
- *Listen to classical music when you're in a car to help your body and your mind relax.*

4

HOW TO DEAL WITH A TRAUMATIC BRAIN INJURY (TBI)

The only true disability in life is a bad attitude.

—Scott Hamilton[1]

You have no idea how much effort I have to put into all that I do.

—Amiee Liz

The part of the brain that allows people to think, to plan, to hope, to dream, to understand language and math, and to recognize themselves and others, is highly malleable.

—Dr. Donalee Markus[2]

Research on traumatic brain injuries caused by car accidents is scant, yet many of the crash survivors I treat suffer from some level of brain injury. As I mentioned in chapter 1, our system of grading a traumatic brain injury as mild, moderate, or severe is inadequate in predicting the level of dysfunction imposed on functionality and quality of life. We may diagnose someone as having a mild TBI, but the impact on their functioning can be *profound*. No brain injury is mild when it comes to the challenges a survivor must cope with. One of the primary sources of head trauma continues to be motor vehicle accidents.[3]

Worldwide, brain injuries and the resulting compromised brain functioning represent a major public health problem. Because the injuries and related compromised functioning, such as memory and reasoning challenges, cannot be easily observed, TBI is called the silent epidemic.[4]

Brain injuries are not well understood by the general public or many healthcare professionals, therefore the injuries often go undiagnosed, unevaluated, and untreated. If there are no fractures or hemorrhages, a brain injury will not show up on an MRI or CT scan. This can lead to challenges for diagnosis and providing evidence of a brain injury to an insurance company.

The economic costs of brain injuries in the United States are enormous in terms of care and lost productivity—estimated at more than $75 billion annually.[5] Brain injuries not attributed to intrinsic factors are called *acquired brain injuries* and are broken into three categories:

1. **Traumatic Impact Injury:** The head is struck by or against an object. It is a *contact injury* resulting in either a nonpenetrating or open penetration impact to the head.

2. **Traumatic Internal Injury:** or *noncontact injury*, which is an aftereffect of the brain moving violently within the skull. The injury results from rotational/angular forces or acceleration/deceleration forces. The injury classification is considered multifocal in which there is what is called *diffuse axonal injury*, *white matter lesions*, or *hemorrhage*. We commonly see traumatic internal brain injuries in falls, automobile accidents, and sports-related injuries.

3. **Coup-Contrecoup Injuries:** The word "coup" is often used in a political context referring to a sudden and violent seizure of power, as in one party illegally overthrowing a government. When applied to brain injuries, it relates to the brain suddenly and violently striking the front of the skull then rebounding and crashing into the back of the head. These violent movements are due to the physical forces of accelera-

tion and deceleration to the brain, which floats in the fluid within the hard, bony structure of the skull.[6]

Injury to the sides of the brain or temporal lobes can result from the head striking the side windows of a vehicle or other objects. The pituitary gland, the master endocrine gland that controls most of our other organs, is anatomically positioned in the brain, so it is vulnerable to injury from rotational forces.[7] The pea-sized pituitary rests in a bony area attached to the base of the brain by a thin stalk and hangs like a miniature punching bag. Forces from a car crash, including airbag deployment, can easily damage the pituitary's delicate vasculature.

The brain comprises about 100 billion nerve cells, all connected by 100 trillion neuro-connections—but who's counting? Because of this complexity, no two brains, nor two brain injuries are the same.

The consequences of a head injury can manifest in an array of complications, which include physical, cognitive, neurobehavioral, psychosocial, and/or occupational. Sometimes, the individual may misuse substances or engage in behaviors that create legal, social, and family difficulties.

Following the primary injury and the initial impact on the brain (which can cause cellular and mechanical damage), delayed nonmechanical, neurochemical processes can occur as secondary injuries.

In the first phase, cellular functioning may be compromised by metabolic imbalances and impaired blood flow that further damages tissue. In the second post-impact phase, further unfolding injury to the brain results from what is termed *axon terminal depolarization*, the release of excitatory neurotransmitters, intracellular breakdown, free radical generation, apoptosis, and necrosis.[8] These technical terms refer to the mechanics of how the brain cells function when sending their chemical messages and the damage of dysregulation of chemical processes or cellular damage. Bottom line, the injury to the brain does not always stop with a knock on the head; there can be a cascade effect set in motion that can continue to damage the brain. The time frame for this continued injury phase is uncertain and can be extended for days, weeks, or months.

The body responds to cellular injury by creating inflammation and activating the immune system to repair impaired tissue. The inflammatory response, which is part of the body's way of healing, causes a side effect of disruption of the brain's neurotransmitters and the ability of the neurons to communicate with one another. The secondary injury phase can cause more tissue damage, which compounds the initial injury to the brain. This is sometimes referred to as the *secondary injury metabolic cascade*.[9] Inflammation involves the release of chemicals from damaged cells, causing leakage and swelling that are not suitable for brain functioning and cell-to-cell communication. This inflammation can severely affect brain functioning and has been linked to chronic activation of the immune system as well as increased risk for dementia in later life. TBI patients are also at increased risk for Alzheimer's disease and suicide.[10]

WHAT IS A CONCUSSION?

A concussion is a head injury or traumatic brain injury. These terms are often used interchangeably. According to the Brain Injury Association of America, a concussion is defined by these four features:

1. Trauma-induced alteration in mental status (dazed, disoriented, confused).
2. A possible loss of consciousness.
3. A memory loss for events immediately before or after trauma.
4. Transient or non-transient local neurological deficits.[11]

If you're diagnosed with a concussion and sent home to rest, it's really important to monitor your symptoms. If you experience any of the following, get to your nearest emergency department:

1. Weakness, numbness, or decreased coordination;
2. A headache that gets worse and does not go away;
3. Repeated vomiting or nausea;

4. Slurred speech;
5. Drowsiness or cannot be awakened;
6. One pupil is larger than the other;
7. Convulsions or seizures;
8. Not recognizing people or places;
9. Becoming increasingly confused, restless, or agitated;
10. Unusual behavior; and/or
11. Loss of consciousness.[12]

WHAT IS IT LIKE TO HAVE A BRAIN INJURY?

"The Cell Phone Won't Charge"

To describe what it's like to have a brain injury, I use the analogy of a cell phone with a battery that won't fully charge. You can only use it for a short period before you must recharge it or it will die, and your ability to communicate with others will abruptly end. Also, neurofatigue can set in shortly after a charge and quickly drains the already low battery.

I know many high-functioning professionals with brain injuries. They can only perform a fraction of the same work that they were able to perform with ease before they sustained neurotrauma. Their ability to mentally function decreases as the day goes on; it's like hitting a brick wall, and they must rest their brains. Often severe headaches are triggered as they attempt to concentrate and focus beyond the shortened attention span caused by their brain injury.

It's important that you know that although a TBI can result in problems with your brain's processing speed, thought processes, memory, attention, focus, learning, reasoning, problem-solving abilities, and speech and language skills, it does *not* affect your level of intelligence.

"There Are Not Enough Spoons"

A friend of mine with a brain injury shared her "spoon theory" with me.[13] Imagine everyone has 20 spoons to use throughout the day. People with healthy brains might use two spoons to get themselves up in the morning and prepare to leave the house to begin a productive workday. When you have a brain injury, it may take 10 or 15 of your spoons just to get out the door, which leaves only a few spoons to get you through the rest of the day.

Fatigue, sleeplessness, slowed information processing, difficulty finding the right words when talking, trouble following conversations, headaches, light and sound sensitivity, irritability, depression, forgetfulness, anxiety, impaired judgment, being accident-prone, having weakened impulse control, and feeling constantly frustrated can all be part of the package. And the kicker? Many people will say, "But you look fine."

NEUROINFLAMMATION AND BRAIN INJURY

A blog I write for *Psychology Today* on topics related to accident trauma, brain injury, and other issues related to suffering and loss led me to become acquainted with Andrew Marr's and Dr. Mark Gordon's work on brain injury and neuroinflammation resulting from blast waves (shock waves from high explosives) in the military. Their work opened my mind to the field of neuroendocrinology and the vital role hormones that play in the body. More than 80 known hormones control different functions of our bodies and minds. This is an area in which most physicians and mental health professionals lack basic knowledge. At various times, psychiatry has been interested in the hormonal basis of mental health conditions but it has turned its back on specific endocrine hormone factors.

A September 2018 white paper (an authoritative perspective report) by Mark L. Gordon, MD, and Andrew Marr titled "A Paradigm Shift in the Diagnosis and Treatment of Symptomatic Trau-

matic Brain Injury (aka PTS/PTSD)," discusses how a traumatic brain injury causes changes in the neurochemistry of the brain due to neuroinflammation.[14] According to the authors, neuroinflammation triggers the release of immune-related cytokines (e.g., IL-1, IL-1b, IL-6, and TNF-alpha). The changes in brain chemistry due to an inflammatory response result in neuron death and create a domino effect. The neurochemistry of the brain further alters and compromises the brain's ability to heal. Dr. Gordon's clinical efforts to address this level of neuroendocrine injury have produced promising results. A hormonal and metabolic screening is recommended for anyone who has sustained a traumatic brain injury. This involves a full blood screening to look at endocrine system function. It's important to note that you can experience endocrine dysfunction even if the hormone values are within what's considered the "normal" range. Dr. Gordon advocates "treating the patient, not the numbers" from the blood results.

Over the years of treating accident survivors, I can now reflect and see many who likely suffered from the effects of hormonal imbalances that resulted from brain injuries that were never diagnosed—or treated. Physicians trained in this area of medicine are few, and unfortunately, they express little interest. The many reasons for this lack of interest are explored in an excellent book, *Endocrine Psychiatry*, by Edward Shorter and Max Fink.[15]

Recently, while taking a brain injury certification course, I met a brilliant physiatrist (physical medicine and rehabilitation physician) from Egypt who had practiced in both Canada and the United States. I asked him why the topic of hormonal imbalances is not addressed more in the United States. He wasn't sure about the United States, but he found that in Canada hormone replacement therapy is commonly used. If this book helps educate the public and healthcare providers about screening for endocrine and metabolic dysfunction, then my efforts will have been worth it.

FRONTAL LOBE SYNDROME

The frontal lobes of the brain are highly evolved neuronal structures that have permitted our civilization to advance to developing language and higher-order thought. Damage to this area of the brain can compromise what we call "executive functioning," which affects how we navigate through life and enables our higher reasoning and problem-solving abilities. Our frontal lobes also help to give us a sense of who we are as distinct human entities. Injury to the front part of the brain can leave us feeling like we are strangers to ourselves.

A famous 1848 case mentioned in most introductory neurology and psychology books involves Phineas Gage who, while working as a railroad foreman, accidentally discharged an explosion that sent a long, iron, tamping rod through the front part of his brain. Incredibly, he survived this injury. After his wounds healed, he could still work, but his personality had changed. He displayed impulsivity and a lack of discretion that led to his losing his job with the railroad. Gage's skull and the tamping rod are on exhibit at Harvard Medical School's Warren Anatomical Museum. [16]

NEUROPLASTICITY

For many years now, we have known that the brain can repair functioning following neurotrauma. This ability is referred to as *neuroplasticity*. Applying the word "plasticity" to human behavior appeared in 1890 in William James's book *The Principles of Psychology.* [17]

We are only just beginning the exciting neuroscientific exploration of the brain and its capacity to heal from injury. For people who have sustained head trauma, there is great hope for recovery with proper treatment. The earlier the injury is diagnosed, the better. We need better diagnostic tools and treatments for TBIs.

Insurance companies funding the diagnostics and treatments needed to facilitate recovery could yield high returns for their businesses. Unfortunately, in my experience, insurance companies are not cooperative with supporting innovative treatments such as hormone replacement therapy for endocrine injuries. This is a shame as until the neurochemistry of the brain is restored, recovery is slow.

When a traumatic brain injury is diagnosed, insurance companies frequently send the "claimant" to neuropsychologists or neurologists who believe they are doing the insurance company a favor by saying there is nothing wrong. Many of these "independent" examiners do not operate ethically and are biased against the injured person. I am not saying all doctors hired by the insurance companies work this way, but sadly, in my experience, many do. Coverage for treatment is then terminated, and you do not get the help you need to recover. This is penny-wise and dollar-dumb insurance industry thinking, not to mention immoral and unethical.

YOUR EYES CONTROL HOW YOU THINK

Dr. Clark Elliott, a professor of artificial intelligence at DePaul University, had what appeared to be a minor rear-end auto crash years ago. Unfortunately, it turned out to be a torturous decade-long struggle to recover from the effects of a traumatic brain injury. Dr. Elliott kept detailed notes of his severely compromised neurocognitive and neurobehavioral functioning and often bizarre symptoms.[18] While he could function at the high level of a university professor, he could only work for short periods (compared with his pre-injury capacity) before the energy in his cognitive battery was drained, and he became incapacitated by neurofatigue.

Examined and treated by many top medical specialists, nothing helped Elliott until he received intervention from two women: one practicing clinically applied neuroscience (Dr. Donalee Markus) and the other neurobehavioral optometry (Dr. Deborah Zelinsky).[19]

Dr. Markus believed that most of the professor's cognitive and motor problems were related to stress on his visual system (sensory input difficulties) resulting from a brain injury. Through work with specific cognitive exercises ("brain puzzles") and customized therapeutic optometric prism lenses provided by Dr. Zelinsky, they facilitated the rewiring of Dr. Elliott's brain around damaged areas and enabled him to regain his personal and professional functioning. Once Dr. Elliott received the interventions needed to heal, his transformation was rapid. Dr. Markus's approach is based on a technique called *mediation*, taken from the theoretical framework of Israeli psychologist Reuven Feuerstein, that intelligence is not fixed and is modifiable—that is, neuroplastic.

Dr. Zelinsky's neuro-optometric rehabilitation approach is based on research that examines the mind-eye connection and the use of therapeutic glasses to facilitate neurological change. Dr. Zelinsky writes in her foreword to Elliott's book that one's retinal pathway to the body affects such critical functions as balance, hormones, neurotransmitters, and many others. She draws from the rich, evidence-based, interdisciplinary field of translational medicine.

The workings of our eyes and ears are primary for our brain's sensory input. It is interesting that when reading to a patient who had sustained an auto-accident-related brain injury, he noticed his vision became blurry when he struggled to concentrate on what he was listening to. We do not usually make the connection between how input to one system may impact the other, but these connections highlight the complexity of functional challenges that can result in injury to the brain.

TBI TREATMENTS

Once a TBI is diagnosed, treatment is focused on neurorehabilitation efforts, which can include psychotherapy, physiotherapy, and occupational, speech, vision, and language therapy. Alongside traditional neurorehabilitation, many of my patients have found non-mainstream treatments that help to alleviate their symptoms and increase their functionality.

Lack of insurance coverage may prohibit you from accessing some of the following potential treatments for your TBI, but the good news is that, with ongoing research and public awareness of brain injury on the rise, nonmainstream treatments are becoming more accessible.

Omega-3s

I recently had the pleasure of speaking with Dr. Michael Lewis, the author of *When Brains Collide: What Every Athlete and Parent Should Know about Concussions and Head Injuries*. He was interested in finding treatments for soldiers with TBI and discovered the effectiveness of the administration of high-dose Omega-3s to reduce inflammation in the brain, increase overall brain health, and act as potential protection from future injury. Similar to neuroendocrinologist Dr. Mark Gordon's approach, he advocates a four-pillar model of care that consists of exercise, nutrition, hormonal balance, and targeted nutritional therapy.[20]

In his book, he highlights the astounding recovery of one of his patients, Grant Virgin, the son of celebrity nutrition and fitness expert J. J. Virgin.

Grant survived a horrific hit-and-run accident that resulted in a torn aorta; severe, multiple brain bleeds; and 13 broken bones. His initial trauma doctor believed he had slim chances of survival. A combination of treatments, including high-dose Omega-3s, and his mother's dedicated efforts, set him on the road to recovery. She wrote an insightful, inspiring book about her experience, titled *Miracle Mindset*, which I highly recommend for all TBI survivors, as well as their families and healthcare providers.

I have worked with many patients who, like Grant, suffered massive physical and physiological traumas from pedestrian crash injuries. Accidents involving pedestrians are tragic reminders of the constant vulnerability to injury and death that all of us face on a daily basis, simply by crossing the road.

Exercise and Dietary Supplements

Along with Omega-3s, many of my patients report symptom improvements with the following supplements: DHA; vitamins D, B12, E, and C; beta-carotene, arnica (directly after the initial injury); MCT oil; probiotics; and acetyl l-carnitine.

A healthy diet including fresh fruit and vegetables, nuts, seeds, and brown rice plays a vital role in healing from bodily trauma and will aid in your brain recovery. It's best to avoid and/or limit sugar, processed foods, alcohol, and caffeine. I have heard that green leafy vegetables, broccoli, walnuts, turmeric, avocado, pineapple, coconut, fish, dark chocolate, and eggs are all excellent in boosting TBI recovery. Naturopaths are good sources of knowledge for everything related to diet, nutrition, healing supplements, and herbs.

In the early days of recovery, your doctor will advise you to focus on rest, but after a few weeks, continuing or starting an exercise regime will aid in your healing. Studies have shown that exercise results in improved cognitive functioning in TBI patients.[21] Exercise will also significantly improve your mood.

Hyperbaric Oxygen Therapy (HBOT)

Somewhat controversial because of potential safety issues and mixed results within the scientific studies to date, HBOT involves lying in a highly pressurized oxygen chamber and breathing in pure oxygen. Many TBI patients who suffer from chronic neurocognitive deficits report significant cognitive improvements after the treatment.[22] It appears that the oxygen therapy helps to heal neurons by providing energy to cells throughout the body, and promoting the growth of new blood vessels in the brain.[23]

Some patients have reported that HBOT helped them years after their initial injury, but there are also studies to suggest that it's most effective earlier in recovery. At this point, HBOT is expensive and not covered by insurance companies. Hopefully that will change in the future with more conclusive evidence on its effectiveness.

A much less concentrated form of oxygen therapy is available in liquid oxygen drops and handheld oxygen canisters. I've heard from patients that both have helped to alleviate some symptoms for brief periods after administration, particularly during high-altitude exposure from airplane travel.

Please note that it is not advisable to fly for at least two weeks after sustaining a concussion.

Meditation and Mindfulness

I am a firm believer in the immense benefits of meditation and mindfulness for stress reduction, relaxation, and overall good mental and physical health. The trauma that both your body and your brain have endured as a result of your injuries makes you more susceptible to stress-related illnesses and mental health disorders. I highly recommend finding programs or courses in your community that teach meditation or mindfulness, making it a daily practice and important part of your recovery journey. There are many great resources online that are easy to access. I've included a few that may help you in the Resources section at the back of this book.

Practicing relaxation techniques, calming your mind, and learning to focus on your breath will help your body and your brain heal.

The Wim Hof Breathing Method

The Wim Hof breathing method can assist you with climbing Mount Everest so you can imagine that it could really help with managing your TBI symptoms! The breathing exercise involves focusing on deep and rhythmic inhalations and exhalations, and leads to increasing your physical and mental abilities to cope with stress. You can find more information on the Wim Hof method in the Resources section at the back of this book.[24]

Craniosacral Therapy (CST)

I was asked by a friend with a TBI to please include some information on craniosacral therapy. She found the treatment hugely beneficial in the first few months after her injury. The pains in her head
decreased, her headaches became more manageable, her sleep quality improved, and her brain fog decreased on the days she had the
treatments.

Craniosacral therapy is generally performed by an osteopath,
massage therapist, or chiropractor and involves the administration
of manipulation and gentle pressure to the joints of the skull, spine,
and parts of the pelvis. The gentle manipulations help to improve
the flow of cerebral spinal fluid and can improve TBI symptoms and
recovery.[25]

Neurofeedback

In 2019, I attended a fascinating conference on neurofeedback,
which resulted in more questions than answers. However, it has
been reported to assist in TBI recovery. The treatment involves the
attachment of electrodes to the patient's head to give them feedback
on the brain's activity. Based on the feedback, the patient then
learns to self-regulate the brain's activity by learning how to affect
the frequency and length of their brainwaves.[26]

Transcranial Magnetic Stimulation (TMS)

TMS is a procedure that involves the use of electromagnetic pulses
that stimulate specific regions of your brain. There are some recent
studies that suggest that TMS may help TBI patients by improving
cognitive function and that it can lead to neurobehavioral gains.[27]

At present, auto insurance companies do not provide coverage
for this treatment, but there is coverage for U.S. military personnel
through Veterans Affairs. It will be interesting to see the results of
future studies on this treatment.

The Future of TBI Treatments

Neuroregeneration and Stem Cell Research

The search for the most effective TBI treatments continues. At our current rate of technological medical advances, I believe that the promising utilization for stem cells in treating TBI is not far off. Research trials are currently underway. One of the most recent trials involved injections of a stem cell product into the site of injury and led to improvements in neurological functioning.[28] The future of neuroregeneration looks promising!

HUMPTY DUMPTY

Humpty Dumpty sat on a wall,
Humpty Dumpty had a great fall.
All the king's horses and all the king's men
Couldn't put Humpty together again.

The Humpty Dumpty rhyme is a powerful metaphor for unforgiving entropy, the second law of thermodynamics—that is, that which was once ordered becomes shattered and disordered.[29] In a child's mind, everything can be repaired, but Humpty Dumpty's fate penetrates this veil of developmental omnipotence and powerfully reminds a child to protect their fragile skull.

As a young child, I cried and felt terrified when I first learned of Humpty Dumpty from my mother. I somehow understood on an existential level that forces in life could destroy what was once integral, whole, and beautiful, and that constant care is needed to prevent such tragic outcomes. Humpty's story created anxiety that helped to keep me safe and reminded me not to do foolish things that might cause me to crack my noggin—or worse. Living with psychological conditions and/or brain injury, you may often feel like poor Humpty and fear that, no matter how great the effort of others, you can never be put back together again.

An artist patient suffered a brain injury from what appeared to be a relatively minor car accident, but like Dr. Elliott, severe neurotrauma affected his functioning. He drew a picture of Humpty Dumpty for me on which I listed many of the common symptoms of traumatic brain injury. I include this drawing in the packet of information I provide to new patients.

Ernest Hemingway offers a counterpart to Humpty Dumpty's entropic, hopeless fate, in one of my favorite quotes: "The world breaks everyone, and afterward, many are strong at the broken places."[30]

Psychotherapy tries to help mend the broken places and perhaps even make them stronger than they were before. Another quote from Hemingway captures what healthcare providers need to remember when working with injured patients. "When people talk, listen completely. Most people never listen."[31] As a car-crash survivor attempting to recover health and a new, postaccident order and functionality, it is essential to surround yourself with professionals and others who will listen to your complaints and the seemingly insurmountable dilemmas the crash wrought upon you.

Helping professionals would be wise to remember that often it is in the listening that a new solution previously unimagined will emerge. The crux of effective psychotherapy cannot be cataloged in a manual.

The effects of car accidents can be a tragic and graphic rendering of Rudolf Clausius's unforgiving second law of thermodynamics. Vehicular crashes deal with excessive transfers of energy that often result in significant disorders, including loss of both equilibrium and cellular integrity. If you have sustained a brain injury, you will know the pain of how it impacts many other systems of order in your world. In an instant, it can feel as though your world has come apart. It often has, and a new order must be created with considerable effort from you and your care providers.

The glue in creating this new order is a positive mind-set, even when that seems impossible. Surround yourself with others who can imagine that what may seem hopeless to you *is* possible, and avoid those who cannot imagine because they are unwilling to do what needs to be done.

TIPS

- *Ask friends and family for help with recording and documenting your symptoms for both your healthcare providers and your insurance company.*
- *If you have a brain injury, be aware of and have compassion for your new limitations. Learn to work around them and give yourself more time to complete tasks. Rest is key.*
- *Brain injury recovery is a process. It takes time. You will have good days and bad days.*
- *While you are healing from a brain injury, you must come to accept your "new normal," which means allowing that, for the time being, you can no longer perform at your pre-injury level. Some skills related to memory may be compromised or lost.*
- *Not all Omega-3s or dietary/herbal supplements are created equally. Research the products on the market and make an informed decision on the products' quality.*

5

A RIVER OF PAIN

Pain is a more terrible lord of mankind than even death itself.
—Albert Schweitzer, MD[1]

A person is, among all else, a material thing, easily torn and not easily mended.
—Ian McEwan[2]

THE RIVER OF PAIN, WOE, AND GRIEF

Acheron, a god in ancient Greek mythology, was transformed into a river of pain, woe, and grief (the Acheron River) by Zeus. The river was said to border Hell and separate the world of the living from the underworld of the dead (Hades). Charon, the ferryman, transported souls from one bank to the other.

For people with chronic pain, the "river of pain, woe, and grief" metaphor is, unfortunately, apt. Often, a disconnect from others and compromised social, recreational, and occupational functioning occur. A wretched thief of sleep, pain leaves the sufferer to toss and turn in hellish nights of insomnia. The ancient Greeks have a way of nailing it every time. The myth of Acheron reminds us that pain is a powerful force and difficult to navigate alone.

Pain is a complex, multifaceted, and subjective phenomena. Even the anticipation of tissue damage to the body can cause pain.[3] There is a famous case of a young construction worker in the United Kingdom who jumped from scaffolding and landed on a large spike that penetrated through the top of his shoe. He was in such excruciating pain that he had to be given morphine just to have his boot cut off at the hospital. Upon removal, it was discovered that the spike had passed between his toes, and there had been no tissue damage. Hence, the power of the mind to create pain.

TYPES OF PAIN

Michael E. Howard, PhD, describes various broad categories of pain: nociceptive, hyperalgesic, neuropathic, psychogenic, and inflammatory.[4] The psychogenic class is defined and driven by psychological factors, therefore it's often dismissed by some medical and insurance professionals. However, studies show that psychological distress can be perceived as physical pain.[5]

Dr. John Sarno was a master at helping chronic pain patients identify the emotional and stress-related roots of pain, leading to its relief.[6] Emotions in 27 distinct categories were identified in recent scientific literature.[7] Anger, fear, disgust, happiness, sadness, and surprise produce unique facial expressions and are thought to represent primary emotions that combine into composite emotions.[8] Sorting out the emotional components of your life can be a complicated process. Psychotherapy can be a literal lifesaver. The title of Karol K. Truman's excellent book, *Feelings Buried Alive Never Die,* captures the clinical reality that often it takes time to explore and unpack our emotions. The more we deposit unprocessed emotions into our mental bank, the more likely they will return, disguised as physical pain symptoms.

Scientific Models of Pain

With their Gate Control Theory, researchers Melzack and Wall were pioneers in the multidimensional perspective of chronic pain.[9] Melzack later integrated his Gate Control Theory with the stress model of Hans Selye in what he termed the *Neuromatrix Theory of Pain*. This theory suggests that pain has multiple influences and has networks of nerve impulses with genetic components that can be modified by learning.[10] Melzack's theory predicts that pain can be triggered either by sensory inputs or centrally (within the brain), without sensory information from the periphery. Both Melzack and Selye indicate that chronic stress can predispose you to develop chronic pain.[11]

One thing my auto-accident trauma patients have in common is pain—chronic pain combined with high stress levels. There are two broad pain classifications: acute and chronic. Acute pain resolves relatively quickly, whereas pain that lasts more than six months is considered chronic. Some of my patients have been struggling with chronic pain for more than two decades. The most common areas are the neck, back, head, and upper and lower extremities.

One fantastic feature of the human body is how it blocks pain signals by releasing chemicals called endorphins. Endorphins are neurochemicals with morphine-like effects. Produced by the hypothalamus, pituitary gland, and the central nervous system, these chemicals are released by the brain when it receives pain signals.

Chronic Pain: The Elephant in the Room

Not all injuries will result in chronic pain, but a great majority do. Chronic pain impacts all aspects of life: occupational, cognitive, social, sexual, and recreational. The overall quality of life can diminish to the point of severe and debilitating depression. Chronic pain and the resulting depression create significant suicide risk factors that should not be ignored. Close clinical monitoring by all members of the interdisciplinary team is needed. People in chronic pain must be open with their treating providers about depression so they can receive the support they need.

One of the best books written on the problem of pain in America is *A Nation in Pain: Healing Our Biggest Health Problem* by health columnist Judy Foreman.[12] The book covers every aspect of chronic pain ranging from the scientific understanding of pain to treatments like marijuana, exercise, and complementary and alternative medicine. Judy calls exercise the "magic bullet for pain" and focuses on studies that show how activity disrupts the downward spiral that pain can trigger when pain sufferers become inactive. (There is a famous quip I use with my patients, "Motion is lotion.") Judy writes from her perspective as a health journalist as well as a chronic pain sufferer, and offers helpful insights to fellow pain victims, policy makers, and healthcare professionals.

Prevalence of Chronic Pain in America

According to the American Chronic Pain Association (ACPA), one-third of Americans suffer from chronic pain with estimated economic cost consequences of $70 billion per year. According to health economists from Johns Hopkins University, the estimated cost of treating pain in the United States is $635 billion per year. An estimated $90 billion is spent on the diagnosis and treatment of low back pain alone.[13]

James Dahlhamer from the Centers for Disease Control and Prevention (CDC) stated, "Pain is a component of many long-lasting conditions, and chronic pain is emerging as a health concern on its own, with negative consequences to individual persons, their families, and society as a whole." Overall, the CDC's report estimated that chronic pain affects 50 million Americans.[14]

Linda Porter, director of the Office of Pain Policy at the National Institute of Neurological Disorders and Stroke, stated, "It is crucial that we fully understand how people's lives are affected by chronic pain. This knowledge will help improve care for individuals living with chronic pain and strategically guide our research programs that aim to reduce the burden of pain at the population level."[15]

Coping with Chronic Pain

Many of my patients suffer from high-impact chronic pain, which substantially limits their ability to function. If you have been injured in a crash, one of the biggest challenges is coping with chronic physical pain. Being proactive and learning to do everything possible—without sinking into addiction or depression—is vital to your survival during the often-long journey to recovery.

This challenge can be often compounded by the mental and emotional aspects of your injury, which are often greater than the physical. Twenty-four centuries ago, Socrates, the ancient Greek philosopher, reminded us that there is no illness of the body that does not create illness in the mind. And Ovid, the Roman poet from 20 centuries ago echoed, "When the mind is ill at ease, the body is affected."

In Michigan, we are subjected to frequent changes in barometric pressure due to lake effects. These numerous and often dramatic shifts (many times within the same day) play havoc on the pain equilibriums of auto-accident survivors. I call this pain *Rain Pain*. It was a wet spring in 2019 in the Detroit area, and all of my patients, including people I know who were not injured in car accidents, complained of back and neck pain.

Frequently, persistent pain attacks one of the most vital parts of our lives—sleep. Many cannot find a comfortable position and sleep fitfully. Pain-related sleep disturbance results in chronic fatigue, which further compromises the ability to function in day-to-day activities. Many surrender their beds and retreat to reclining chairs for some level of relief and, at least, a few hours of sleep. Some turn to combinations of sleep medications, marijuana, and CBD preparations.

According to a 2012 National Institute of Health survey, 19 percent of patients with chronic pain seek complementary treatments such as natural health products, and mind-body exercises such as deep breathing, Tai Chi, Yoga, and Qigong, which are thought to have a positive effect on body functioning via the nervous system's influence on the endocrine and immune systems.[16] These practices also help to restore a sense of control over the body and release mood-enhancing neurochemicals. Such alternative and complementary approaches are gaining popularity and media attention.

Fibromyalgia

Chronic pain is a key feature of fibromyalgia, along with fatigue, depression, anxiety, sleep disturbance, migraines, and mental fog. It is a difficult condition to diagnose as symptoms can overlap with many other conditions. Physical or emotional traumas, including auto-accident trauma, and PTSD have been linked to the condition.[17] It is not uncommon for car-crash survivors to develop fibro symptoms many years after the crash.

Pain and Relationship Issues

If you suffer from chronic pain and sleep with a partner, behaviors such as tossing and turning or retreating to a recliner may create issues at home. Your relationship often takes a backseat to your injuries. This can create anxiety, resentment, and confusion for everyone involved. Communication is key. Keep talking about how postaccident circumstances affect everyone. Listen without judging. Just being heard can give relief.

Good sleep hygiene practices are really important in helping to stay on top of your pain. Please see the sleep hygiene tips in the Resources section at the back of this book.

PAIN IS SUBJECTIVE

Car crashes frequently result in what is medically called *polytrauma* involving internal, peripheral nerve, and soft-tissue injuries. These can be challenging to diagnose and can take a long time to heal. An even more disturbing fact is that there's no accurate way of measuring pain as it is a subjective experience.

Typically, we ask patients to rate their pain on a scale of zero for no pain to 10, which is the worst pain possible. In a cruel twist, insurance companies often demand objective evidence of your injuries and your progress. There is no easy way to provide "objective" evidence for pain—be it physical or mental—which often leads to insurance adjusters denying coverage for care if their conscience permits or their managers demand it.

Insurance companies' Independent Medical Examination (IME) physicians are prone to dismiss auto-accident conditions as "just soft-tissue" injuries and declare subjective pain ratings as exaggerations. But pain and compromised functioning from soft-tissue injuries can be disabling and fuel high levels of depression, anxiety, and loss of quality of life.

POSITIONAL MRIs

Regular Magnetic Resonance Imaging (MRI) does not capture all injuries. However, some MRI companies use scan techniques that involve flexion, extension, and rotation of the head that can reveal problems that run-of-the-mill imaging studies miss, such as disc herniation and indicators of edema and inflammation associated with tissue tears. There are also companies that can do a 3-D reconstruction rendering of the injured area.

I asked a friend, Jodi Coden, for more information about imaging issues. As director of physician relations for M1 Imaging, Jodi is uniquely qualified to articulate some difficult-to-obtain information about the benefits of MRI imaging. Her company uses the flexion/extension technique to see if there is spinal cord compression or increased herniation, and thus more pain when the patient's neck is in a bent position. They use a positioning technique called "alar protocol" that angles the neck in a way that allows them to see any additional pathology that would otherwise be unnoticeable in a supine (flat) position.

By looking at alar protocol images, a treating physician can see if there are any ligament tears between cervical spinal disks C1 and C2. Any tears could jeopardize the patient's movement capability if treatment occurs on an undetected rip. For example, if a partial or full tear is present and a chiropractor adjusts the neck, a patient could become catastrophically injured. A complete bilateral tear could even have fatal consequences.

Through this type of imaging, we can establish whether patients are safe candidates for prescribed treatments. Jodi explained that because auto injuries are extremely complicated survivors require advanced imaging before beginning any treatment.

TIPS

- *Some insurance companies will pay for a recliner, special pillows, or a specific bed if your pain specialist writes a prescription/recommendation for it.*
- *Find the best pain management and rehabilitation treatment provider to orchestrate your overall recuperation plan, pain management recommendations, and referrals. In the United States, these specialized physicians are called PM&Rs (Physical Medicine and Rehabilitation) or physiatrists (not to be confused with psychiatrists).*
- *Know that there are many pain management alternatives to surgery and pain medications that are just as, or even more effective, without the risks or side effects.*
- *Because insurance company adjusters and attorneys know a jury would better understand your injuries when they see a graphic reconstruction, 3-D reconstruction renderings can be a powerful litigation tool. When it comes to tools to use to support your injury documentation, a 3-D reconstruction rendering can be a bazooka.*

6

MANAGING YOUR PAIN

Father, if thou be willing, remove this cup from me: nevertheless not my will, but thine, be done.

—Luke (AKJV 22:42)

THE CYCLE OF PAIN

Dr. Martin T. Taylor, a neurologist and professor at the Ohio College of Osteopathic Medicine, wrote an excellent resource book for anyone with chronic pain from neck and back injuries. In *My Neck Hurts! Nonsurgical Treatments for Neck and Upper Back Pain*, Taylor describes the "Cycle of Pain" seen in people who suffer long-term pain difficulties.[1] Pain leads to depression and anxiety, which leads to sleep problems and fatigue, resulting in more pain. On and on the cycle persists. Without interruption, this vicious cycle can push people to severe distress. The sense of profound helplessness that your pain creates can be devastating. But it can also be conducive to developing some control and self-agency when you are armed with the right information and professionals to guide you. There are a plethora of pain management specialists and treatment providers outside of your primary care physician to assist you in healing your injuries and managing your pain. They include physical therapists, orthopedic specialists and surgeons, neurologists, physiatrists, rheumatologists, acupuncturists, chiropractors, and massage therapists.

Dr. Martin Taylor's Table of Contents maps many of your treatment options ranging from noninvasive to more involved nonsurgical options such as the following:

1. Noninvasive treatment options:

    - TENS (transcutaneous electrical nerve stimulation)
    - OMT (Osteopathic Manipulative Treatment)
    - counseling
    - yoga
    - Pilates
    - acupuncture
    - aqua therapy
    - heat and ice
    - cervical traction
    - massage
    - biofeedback

2. Types of medications used:

    - NSAIDs (aspirin, ibuprofen)
    - muscle relaxants
    - opioids
    - oral steroids
    - antidepressants
    - antiseizure medications
    - topical creams or patches

3. Injections and more invasive procedures:

    - TPI (trigger point injections)
    - botulinum toxin injections (Botox)
    - epidural injections

- facet/medial branch blocks or denervation
- occipital nerve blocks
- spinal cord stimulation
- prolotherapy (injection of a natural irritant into a joint's interior)[2]

Similar to prolotherapy, a therapy called PRP involves the injection of your own platelet-rich blood plasma into the injured area. It's a relatively new therapy being used to treat musculoskeletal conditions, including lower back pain. Most recent studies have found that it is effective. I have heard reports that it works in reducing pain for months at a time, but it does require repeat injections.[3]

A more invasive procedure that Taylor describes as giving extended temporary relief is Radiofrequency Ablation (RFA). RFA, also known as a rhizotomy, destroys a facet joint's sensory nerve with a heat probe. Each facet joint has two nerves that carry pain signals from the joints to the spine and brain. Often, it takes several weeks for the benefits of the procedure to lead to full pain relief, which can last months or even years. The nerves eventually grow back, the pain returns, sometimes to previous levels, and the RFA can be repeated.

I have patients who undergo dozens of RFA procedures, helping them maintain a significant level of functionality. Severe pain is easier to accept if you know a measure of relief is available, even if it is only partial and temporary. RFA is performed, under full or local anesthetic in the cervical, thoracic, or lumbosacral facets (joints in the spine), by pain specialists, and often by physiatrists or orthopedic spine specialists.[4]

A research study reported that the use of general anesthesia for RAF shortens the operating time and the patient's discomfort without impairing success rate.[5] (Note: If you are also dealing with the effects of a brain injury, you can be more sensitive to anesthesia and experience lingering brain fog after the procedure. The whole person and all of their conditions must be considered when weighing treatment options.)

RAF is often helpful in treating such pain conditions as failed back surgery syndrome, complex regional pain syndrome, and peripheral nerve entrapment.[6]

THE USE OF OPIOIDS

Bill's Pain Story

At 18, Bill was ejected from a car on the expressway in a high-speed crash. The driver, his girlfriend, died instantly, and Bill suffered severe injuries to his head and back. For years, opioids were prescribed for his pain until the government cracked down on prescribers. Bill gradually turned to heroin after finding prescription pain medications too expensive and difficult to obtain. One night, he and a friend overdosed. Another friend discovered them and contacted emergency services. Naloxone was administered to both. On the third administration of naloxone, Bill regained consciousness. His friend was unresponsive to the naloxone and died.

Bill now struggles to resolve his grief from both deaths while attempting to live an opioid-free life. He attends Narcotics Anonymous five days a week and is active in group psychotherapy, where he gains the support he needs to continue on. Creating new friendships with nondrug users and eliminating those who still use has also been vital. After successfully completing a three-month residential treatment program, he is a healthy weight and, for the first time since the crash, is drug and alcohol free. He is learning again what it's like to feel his emotions and is slowly accepting that it's safe to do so.

The Opiate Epidemic

Naloxone (brand names Narcan or Evzio) can treat a narcotic overdose in an emergency. According to the National Institute on Drug Abuse (NIDA), naloxone is a significant weapon in the epidemic of opioid overdoses in the United States. More than 115 Americans die every day from opiate overdoses. According to James J. Galligan, a professor of pharmacology and toxicology at Michigan State University, naloxone works by binding to opioid receptors and reversing or blocking the effects of opioids. Many emergency responders are now required to carry naloxone with them to use for patients who have overdosed.[7]

Unfortunately, the safety of narcotic pain medications was oversold to physicians in the United States. According to the CDC (Centers for Disease Control and Prevention), nearly 220,000 people died from overdoses on prescription narcotic drugs from 1999 to 2017.[8] The most recent tragic and grim statistics from 2017 show opiate overdose deaths surpassing the number of auto-crash deaths.[9]

Restrictions regarding narcotic medication prescribing began with guidelines issued by the CDC in 2016. Some say these guidelines have been grossly misinterpreted by politicians and were mainly directed at primary care physicians who were overprescribing narcotics and lacked specialization in pain management.

Fifteen or so years ago, when I began giving specialized care to auto-accident patients, opiates were frequently prescribed to manage long-term, chronic pain. Drug company representatives informed physicians that opioids were safe for extended pain management, and drug company conferences beat the drum. The emphasis has now dramatically shifted to non-opiate treatment. Opiates are now used in limited quantity to treat postsurgical pain. Many U.S. states have now enacted new opioid laws. Some have imposed laws that limit the maximum dose for most patients and placed restrictions on what could be prescribed and for how long, and some exempt prescribing except by board-certified pain specialists. In Michigan, prescribers of pain medication are now required to have monthly follow-ups with their patients.

The abrupt shift in pain medication prescribing has left many patients in a crisis. With prescription opiates abruptly withdrawn, many addicted patients still dealing with severe, chronic pain turn to street drugs. A statistic released from the CDC showed that from 2016 to 2017, there was at least a 45 percent increase in death rates linked to synthetic opioids (most likely from illicitly manufactured fentanyl). Debra Houry, MD, director of the CDC's National Center for Injury Prevention and Control, reported that the drug overdose epidemic, involving many types of drugs such as opioids, cocaine, and psycho stimulants, continues to increase.[10]

Led by the U.S. Department of Health and Human Services (HHS), the government is implementing a five-point strategy to address the epidemic. This includes better treatment, better data, better research, better pain management, and increased access to naloxone.

THINKING OUTSIDE THE PAIN MANAGEMENT BOX

David Hanscom, a spine surgeon practicing for more than 30 years, believes that up to 80 percent of spine surgeries are unnecessary.[11] Hanscom encourages stress management approaches that look for and release unresolved emotional issues that may play a pain-related role. His approach is like that of renowned PM&R physician and New York University School of Medicine professor John Sarno, who successfully treated many celebrities and luminaries that suffered from chronic pain.[12] You can see a YouTube video of Dr. Sarno testifying about chronic pain before a United States Senate hearing.[13]

Sarno helped a sitting senator eliminate his back pain without resorting to surgery, despite recommendations by three of the nation's top surgeons. Howard Schubiner is an excellent physician and professor of medicine in the Detroit area who also practices mind-body medicine, which draws on the work of John Sarno.[14]

Sarno's, Hanscom's, and Schubiner's perspectives have moved beyond the strictly biomedical model that began with ancient Greek physicians and has dominated medical education since the time of Descartes in the 17th century. The biopsychosocial and mind-body perspectives offer many advantages to the narrow, body-only approach that has permeated American medicine since World War II.

MIGRAINES: THE EMOTIONAL AND STRESS CONNECTION

Many patients mention that the onset of a migraine headache is triggered when they have extended themselves beyond their fatigue level. When a person pushes beyond their limits, cognitive collapse begins to set in, and the ability to focus and concentrate nosedives into a blinding headache. Debilitating migraines are often accompanied by nausea, vomiting, photophobia (light sensitivity), and phonophobia (sound sensitivity). Migraines are frequently activated when sufferers feel overwhelmed and can't manage life's stressors. Other common emotional triggers for migraines are anger and its sister emotion, frustration. Post-crash, there is an abundant supply of situations ripe for producing frustration. Therefore, your stress management is crucial to recovery and positivity. There are several pain management options for migraines, including Botox, over-the-counter analgesics, beta blockers, and massage therapy. Ask your doctor or neurologist for suggestions.

Try to manage your stress by engaging in self-care strategies such as taking a walk, having a relaxing bath, listening to tranquil music, meditating, doing yoga or Pilates, taking a dance or Zumba class, sitting by a beautiful body of water, spending time with your pets, and practicing deep-breathing techniques.

One of the great relaxation masters, Belleruth Naparstek, is a guided imagery pioneer. Because of Naparstek, I have learned how to induce patients into a deep state of relaxation. She has a library of different guided imagery programs on topics like preparing for surgery, overcoming PTSD, and dealing with grief, all available to purchase or stream online. As a transcendental meditation practitioner for more than 40 years, I have discovered that Naparstek's guided imagery induces a state of calm similar to deep meditation. Try it! Maybe you will be like one of the 95 percent of my patients who find it beneficial! I have included links to her work in the Resources section at the back of this book.

OTHER TOOLS FOR MANAGING PAIN

Lost Healing

I now practice in Mount Clemens located about 30 minutes from Detroit on the Clinton River. From the 1870s to about 1940, Mount Clemens was a world-famous spa city with more than 30 hotels and bathhouses. The mineral baths were reported to treat more than 40 conditions—particularly joint and back pain. The healing water came from a 600-million-year-old underground sulfuric aquifer that contained more than 30 minerals. [15] Due to the Great Depression and the rise of pharmaceuticals, the mineral bath industry collapsed in Mount Clemens. Sadly, the mineral wells are now sealed over with concrete and asphalt.

Nature has always provided us with healing resources! It's important to listen to your own body's intuitive, natural requests for healing and managing pain. Holistic healing techniques involve you or your treatment provider harnessing intuition. The ancient, holistic practices of Reiki and reflexology have also been found to reduce and manage pain and are worth exploring.

Journal Writing

Journal writing is also a powerful tool to try for your pain management. Julia Cameron's book, *The Artists Way,* describes three self-care tools for creatives: (1) a daily 20-minute walk, (2) daily journal writing without editing, and (3) a weekly date to do something you typically deprive yourself of. [16] (As an example, I gave myself an "artist date" yesterday. I visited a second-hand store for a 15-minute window-shop. Even though my work schedule easily justified passing the store, the short minivacation I took on the way back from the post office relieved my stress considerably. After clearing my head by indulging in this short, relaxing activity, the long list of things I needed to do seemed less stressful, and the rest of my day flowed more easily.)

The Power of Beliefs

Our beliefs really can heal us or kill us. The Holocaust survivor Viktor Frankl was a young psychiatrist when imprisoned in Auschwitz. Through his experiences, he discovered the life-preserving importance of having purpose and meaning. He survived by learning his purpose, which was to perform at least one act of compassion each day. It could be something small like sharing a scrap of bread or helping someone do a chore. By consciously doing this practice, he grew stronger. In contrast, he discovered the power of failed belief. Often rumors would circulate around the concentration camp that liberation by the Allies would occur on a specific date. When that date passed and the Allies failed to arrive, those who strongly believed the rumors would often become ill and die within days.[17]

Hypnosis and the Placebo Effect

Hypnosis is effective as a pain management tool because it can facilitate the release of endorphins.[18] Military field surgeons have, when necessary, relied on this and placebo treatments to perform surgery without anesthesia. Having run out of morphine, they would tell the patient about to undergo surgery that they were receiving a powerful painkiller when, in fact, they were injected with saline. For an excellent examination of the placebo effect, see Dr. Joe Dispenza's book, *You Are the Placebo*.[19]

Mainstream medicine has traditionally denigrated the importance of placebo techniques—perhaps because it is difficult to monetize—and believing in the techniques is challenging for many physicians. An exception is Dr. Herbert Benson, a Harvard cardiologist and one of the pioneers in mind-body medicine. Benson prefers the term "remembered wellness" when talking about placebos. His book *The Relaxation Response* became the number one self-help book prescribed by clinical psychologists as an adjunct to psychotherapy.[20]

Dr. Bruce H. Lipton explores the topic of placebo beliefs in his fascinating book, *The Biology of Belief*. Lipton, a pioneering cell biologist, studied epigenetics and stem cells. He noted that the human body is composed of 50 trillion cells performing more than 100,000 different chemical reactions per minute. These reactions orchestrate and coordinate trillions of neural connections and activities. Beliefs can determine how these activities operate. He discusses how beliefs formed before age seven are downloaded from our caregivers and continue to run as subconscious, automatic programs.[21] Psychotherapy can help to ferret out the subconscious programs that create dysfunction and pain in our lives.

TIPS

- *Explore all non-opioid pain management treatment options with your healthcare providers. If you think you may be addicted to opioids, speak to your doctor and reach out to resources within your community such as Narcotics Anonymous.*
- *Find a mind-body program in your area.*
- *Try using Epsom salts in the bath, or if you can, spend time in mineral baths or hot springs to help ease your pain.*
- *Think about and implement the practical stress management tools you relied on before you were injured.*

7

POSITIVE PSYCHOLOGY

Everything can be taken from a man but one thing: the last of the human freedoms—to choose one's attitude in any given set of circumstances, to choose one's own way.

—Viktor Frankl[1]

Psychology is not just the study of weakness and damage; it is also the study of strength and virtue. Treatment is not just fixing what is broken; it is nurturing what is best within us.

—Martin E. P. Seligman[2]

CASE EXAMPLE: MOLLY

Molly has allowed me to share her story of car-accident trauma and the challenges it first presented. Her experience shows the "ground zero" effects of a crash and the great distance that must be traveled to regain emotional and mental balance post–traumatic incident.

"I was passing through a green light when I heard an enormous *bang*. All the airbags in my car deployed, and for a few moments, blocked my vision. The car whirled across the intersection and came to rest in front of a restaurant. The steering column of my vehicle started to smoke, so I knew I'd better get out before I inhaled the toxic chemicals.

"My heart palpitated, my left ear became plugged, and my head rang. Although I couldn't control my shaking, I made my way around to the rear of the car. A waiter from the restaurant rushed to my side and held me steady. He called 911, and in minutes, I was in an ambulance. I was in shock, and my mind kept searching for answers to what had just happened. After waiting in the emergency room—which took hours—I finally saw a doctor. She said there were no broken bones, asked me more questions, and checked my left ear. She mentioned it was red inside and asked if I wanted a CT scan, but I just wanted to go home.

"My mind kept going to the green light. I was only minutes from my home when, in an instant, my life changed. I didn't even know what happened. At home, I had a bowl of soup and tried to figure out what to do next. My brain seemed foggy, so I watched some TV and went to bed.

"When I awoke the next morning, I first asked myself, 'What day is it?' I had things to do and people who depended on me. My ears rang, and the left one was still plugged. There was pain in my neck muscles and shoulders, and my head felt like I had been badly shaken. 'My car!! I have to find my car.' As if a hammer had smacked my head, a hard reality set in.

"I called the police who said that my car had been towed. There was no police report yet; it would probably take several days. The hospital wanted me to fill out some reports with claim numbers from the insurance company. The insurance claims representative I spoke with was pleasant and gave me the information I needed for the hospital.

"I called the towing company who said I owed them $300.00 to get my car out of their lot. A case manager from the insurance company told me some legal things that had to happen. By this time, I knew I couldn't go to work. I was too sore, and my brain wasn't working right. I texted everyone I had planned to meet with and canceled.

"Later that day, my friend took me to the tow yard. When I saw the front end of my car, I cried. I loved my car; she had a special meaning to me. I sobbed when I learned she was totaled. I had to remove the license plate and my things. She had a full tank of gas and a new oil change. What a waste. I had taken such good care of her, and she had been so good to me—protected me from even more severe injuries. We had to find a junkyard to take her to—her final resting place.

"I cried for the rest of the day—grief for my car and gratefulness the accident wasn't any worse than it was. I was still walking around and breathing. That was all I was doing though. My neck and shoulder muscles ached, my head hurt, and now there was pain in my lower back. I couldn't concentrate, was confused, and couldn't remember what I was doing. Making a decision seemed impossible, so I sat down and brushed the cat until she grew tired of that and pushed me away.

"The next morning, I woke up wanting to go to work but couldn't. I worried about lost income, but could do nothing. My head hurt and muscles ached. I tried to review e-mails but found I couldn't concentrate. Then the cat reminded me I needed to clean the litter box.

"I spent the rest of the day wandering around the house and sitting with the infrared heating pad. I felt angry and lost. My mobility had been taken away. If you don't have transportation, you're stuck. What was I going to do about a car? I squeaked by on a fixed income and couldn't just go buy a new vehicle.

"The next day, I tried to remember how to make the breakfast drink I have every morning. The phone rang—an appointment that I had overlooked canceling. I missed a scheduled meeting. I never forgot things like that. Although the woman was understanding, I felt like a fool.

"My ear was still plugged; my head continued to ring and hurt. My shoulders and neck were still stiff and sore, and my arms felt like noodles hanging off my shoulders. I had to concentrate if I wanted to move them. At least the sun was shining, and I was still here to see it! I wanted to garden but couldn't. This was hard; I'm a person who stays busy. I had a difficult time speaking in complete sentences, and I wished my brain worked.

"Time passed. It has been three weeks since the crash! I thought I would be so much better by now, but I'm NOT! I've tried to get past this. I feel so isolated. My friends are kind and offer to help, but I don't want to need help. Before the crash, I was happy, healthy, social, creative, and had a very positive outlook on life. Now, I hurt constantly, my head aches, and I quiver inside. My doctor told me I shouldn't read, watch TV, look at the computer or my phone, or do any close-up work. What's left? I wander around and look at the flowers I'd planted earlier in the spring. They used to bring me such JOY. . . . I miss that feeling. Will it ever return?

"My doctor prescribed steroids for the concussion and whiplash. They made me feel worse. I can't sleep. I'm not a crier, but I lie in bed and sob. Where is this coming from? My eyes aren't working as well as they used to. Everything is blurry. It takes me an entire day to do a task that would typically take me an hour to complete.

"My artistic ability seems to have vanished. This constant noise in my head drives me insane . . . and my ears are still plugged, and the ringing from the *boom* of the airbags exploding all around keeps bombarding me. The other day, I stood in the yard to enjoy the flowers and the fountain, and a loud *bang* came from somewhere. I nearly jumped out of my skin. It was just the sound of a neighbor slamming the lid to his grill, but it took me a while to slow my heart rate and catch my breath.

"So, it's 2 a.m., I can't sleep, and I'm sitting here writing. I hope it will help get some of these feelings of frustration out. I'm tired and exhausted. My mind keeps going back to the crash. I am flooded with 'what ifs' and 'if onlys.' The sighing, crying, quivering, and spasms won't stop. My stomach grumbles, yet I don't feel like eating. Please tell me this will all go away.

"I had spent the last year working on myself. My physical, emotional, and spiritual outlook was good. Well, perhaps if I hadn't, this whole thing would have been much worse. No broken bones, which is something to be grateful for. But all these doctor appointments.

Can't they just tell me how to fix it? I don't want their pharmaceuticals!

"'It takes time,' they say.

"But how much more time do I have? Time is one's most precious commodity, and it is being drained from me! And I just saw how it could all end in an instant.

"What if I have to give up my work? I spent years developing a successful business. It is my passion. I cry some more. My stomach feels twisted. My neck sends shooting pains into my head. My eyes feel dry and gritty. The cat sits and looks at me like, 'Why aren't we sleeping?' My muscles are tense. Every loud noise makes me jump, and every fast movement frightens me. Sighing and crying! Is that all I can do?

"Too many thoughts race through my head. The guy charged through a red light and changed my life. My joyful life altered in the blink of an eye. *Boom*! Just like that. The little girls from next door come over for chocolate chip cookies. They are so sweet, but this evening, when I saw them in my yard, I hid! I buy cookies just for them. I have the cookies, but I hide? What sense does that make? This is not me. What is happening? It is 3 a.m. My alarm is set for 6 a.m. Maybe I should try to go to bed again."

GLASS HALF FULL

I grew up hearing the rhetorical phrase, "Is the glass half empty or half full?" Your answer reflects your worldview. If you see the glass as half empty, you may have a pessimistic worldview. You might believe things only get worse. Whereas, if you see the glass as half full, you may be an optimist with an abundance of inner resources and no need to worry.

There are several well-known ambiguous images that can be perceived as two different things. One of the most famous images shows, depending on your perception, either the profile of an attractive young woman with a feather in her hair, or from a different perspective, a grim older woman with a scarf around her head.[3]

Psychology's field of perception research often uses these optical illusions. A rabbit-duck drawing published in an 1892 German magazine, *Fliegende Blatter*, shows a rabbit looking to the right or a duck looking to the left.[4] Books of these ambiguous images are fun to look at and make for delightful food for the brain.

Our brains are wired to visually register the angles in images and then process the angles to create a complete picture of what they mean. The *Gestalt* concept—the sum of the parts is greater than the whole—uses the German word meaning "pattern" or "configuration." When you have been traumatized from a car crash, your brain looks for patterns and cues to determine if you are safe or in danger of being hurt again.

For example, the sound of something slamming on a hardwood floor can signal your amygdala (a brain structure that processes emotions) to generate intense anxiety. The loud sound and intense anxiety can signal your brain's memory bank to spew out a terrifying image of the semitruck that T-boned your car and came within inches of killing you. You may re-experience the sensory impressions of the shock waves that traveled through your body from the impact.

In processing trauma, it's as if our brain looks at the pieces of a puzzle and, in a nanosecond, creates "a whole" picture from the pieces. We can experience a startle response inappropriate for the stimulus, and the image created may not be real. We must shift our perception to see that it is really a duck and not a rabbit. My mentor, psychoanalyst and traumatologist Henry Krystal, always reminded me of the three rules of trauma and emotion:

1. Feelings are not facts.
2. Feelings are temporary.
3. Feelings are not dangerous.

David J. Morris's fascinating book *The Evil Hours: A Biography of Post-Traumatic Stress Disorder*, mentioned in chapter 3, discusses what's called *apophenia*.[5] Apophenia is the human impulse to find patterns in life. Morris explains how NASA studied photographs of the formation on Mars that appeared to be a human face, but when the lighting changed, it looked more like a glob of cookie dough. The word "apophenia" refers to mistaken perceptions and meanings attributed to unrelated things.

When we survive events that threaten to rob us of life or limb, we must help our brain rewire itself and not fall victim to apophenia. We have to constantly reassure ourselves that the new sound that created anxiety is not the same sound we heard in the crash. Seeing the differences, not the similarities, is the key. It is necessary to exercise our brains and perceptional processes in the same way we would exercise our arms to make the muscles stronger.

Positivity researcher Barbara L. Fredrickson writes that our mind-set alters the way our brains work. Positivity expands our perception and allows us to see more options and opportunities for growth.[6]

A Holocaust survivor, Yisrael Kristal, lost his wife and two children in Auschwitz. He then remarried and had more children. At his 100th birthday celebration, his son described his father as always finding the positive in every situation. Yisrael lived until age 113!

As you recover from your injuries, it may be a real challenge to stay optimistic—to always look for the positive in every situation as Yisrael Kristal did. Another proverbial expression, "Every cloud has a silver lining," reminds us to look for the positive in a negative event. In Alcoholics Anonymous, the Serenity Prayer invites people to accept circumstances in life that are outside of their control and provides them with an internal sense of agency. "God grant us the serenity to accept the things we cannot change, the courage to change the things we can, and the wisdom to know the difference."[7]

When reminders of your crash trigger you, your nervous system goes into emergency mode and screams, "Battle stations! We are under attack; fight for your life!" When this happens, pull back; remember to breathe and take some time out. These alarm reactions are normal and will pass.

Talk with an understanding person about your emotional responses. This will help you to process your emotions so you are not hijacked by the survival mechanisms of your mind and body. Focus on maintaining a calm state of mind, and when your nervous system gets activated, you will have considerable inner resources to manage it. Giving and receiving hugs from your loved ones helps too and can actually reduce levels of the stress hormone cortisol in your body!

My young son recently wrote me a simple note, "Think positive. Live positive." To use it as a reminder to live a full and abundant life, I taped it to the cover of the notebook I kept while writing this book. In the words of Mahatma Gandhi,

> *Your thoughts become your words*
> *Your words become your actions.*
> *Your actions become your habits.*
> *Your habits become your values.*
> *Your values become your destiny.* [8]

As much as we might try, we cannot always control what happens to us. We can, however, strive to control our thoughts and reactions to the events we encounter in life. I love the quote that many attribute to Carl Jung, "I am not what happened to me. I am what I choose to become." The quote is inspiring, yet challenging to put into practice, particularly with trauma-induced apophenia distorting your thinking and twisting your perceptions. For example, you may find it difficult not to have a physiological reaction when a large truck passes by you on the highway if you had been in an accident where a semitruck had sideswiped you. The vehicle may be entirely in its lane, but your mind perceives it as veering ever closer to crossing the dividing line.

Dr. Jennifer Sweeton wrote how trauma impacts the brain in three central ways:

1. The thinking center of the brain, the prefrontal cortex, becomes underactivated.
2. The emotional regulation center, the anterior cingulate cortex, becomes underactivated.
3. The fear center, the amygdala, becomes overactivated. [9]

She described psychotherapy, which supports your work to change your brain through the ingredients of effort, repetition, and time, as the best gift you can give yourself. "Brain training" will help you to better cope with your emotional responses. She also recommends adding a body- and mindfulness-based practice to your daily routine.

Psychologist and Pepperdine University professor Louis Cozolino suggests that the effective psychotherapist is an amygdala whisperer who works diligently with the patient to turn down the overactive fear center in their brain.[10] Once the overactive fear response is decreased, the thinking and emotional regulation centers can then reactivate, regain dominance, and restore homeostasis. Again, meditation, guided imagery, and yoga are powerful tools to achieve a relaxation response that can restore a positive attitude.

Neuroendocrinologist Dr. Mark L. Gordon talks about helping the injured brain heal by creating a "neuro-permissive" environment for recovery with hormone replacement therapy and nutraceuticals. Effective psychotherapy also helps create a neuro-permissive environment by establishing a space of inner peace that turns off the fear-induced stress hormones and enables the release of serenity-type hormones.

We first learn about overcoming agitated states in childhood when we are soothed in various ways by our caregivers. As adults, we must learn to comfort ourselves. Mindfulness practices as prescribed by Jon Kabat-Zinn (founder of MBSR—mindfulness-based stress reduction) and many others can help us achieve mental states of calmness and cultivate serenity regardless of what is happening around us. The word "calm" has origins in the Latin word *cauma*, which refers to a time when everyone finds a place to rest from the oppressive midday heat. We must work to be gentle with ourselves and calm in the storms of life, be they inner or outer. Focus on the positive, moment to moment.

TIPS

- *Every day, think of five things you are grateful for. It can be as simple as being grateful that the sun is shining. Develop an attitude of gratitude!*
- *Repeat positive affirmations to yourself while you're having a bath or shower.*
- *Smile at the next person you pass on the street. Not only has research found that smiling lowers stress and boosts your mood, there's also a good chance that they will smile back!*

8

THE POWER OF EMPATHY

Attention is love.
Holding tenderly and with great affection;
The sensations in the body.
Listening to the call,
Attending to their simple truth
Of feeling.

Sharing is an act of love.
Listening is a form of risk.
Emotions speak through the body.
When we listen deeply,
We can touch the sound of truth.

—Robert Weisz, PhD[1]

Empathy is the capacity to feel and understand what another person is experiencing and the ability to put yourself in their shoes. The qualities and traits associated with empathy have allowed our species to survive. Empathy is closely related to compassion, kindness, and understanding—the emotions that create a neuropermissive environment for healing. If you are in recovery, try to surround yourself with people and professionals who possess these traits. The need to receive empathy is one reason a person sees a psychotherapist.

If you are severely injured in a car wreck, your life is held in the hands of the professionals who will treat you. Take care in selecting your team by choosing specialists who are highly skilled and who care about you as an individual. They should be your advocates and want the best for you for reasons beyond receiving payment for their services.

THE TRAUMA RESERVOIR

Earlier in this book, I quoted Hemingway with "the world breaks everyone, and afterward, many are stronger at the broken places."[2] We cannot go through life without being touched by trauma and loss. Many feel "broken" for a time. But remember, you are not your injury, condition, or diagnosis. We grow by facing challenges and learning to overcome them. If you feel crushed by these challenges, know that there are resources and professionals who can help to relieve the burden. By conquering these challenges, you will become stronger.

I gave a presentation at a brain injury conference recently and showed a slide of two dogs—one three feet tall and the other only ten inches off the ground—both standing in mud. The caption read, "How deep is the mud?" The answer depends on who you ask. Just as no two injuries are the same, everyone's capacity to cope with trauma differs, and everyone's ability to cope with a specific stressor varies depending on their circumstances.

Dr. Robert Weisz, a clinical psychologist, posted a presentation on YouTube in which he discusses the "trauma reservoir."[3] Imagine a container within your mind that holds all of the unresolved emotions connected with the traumatic events that you've experienced throughout your life. There are small traumas (with a little *t*) comprising relatively minor incidents that upset you but nevertheless cause significant stress in your life, and there are big traumas (with a big *T*).

Example

You are the victim of identity theft, and it takes months of effort and expense to restore your credit. During this process, you discover that some banking professionals could care less about your problems. Or maybe your business partner betrays you, and you need a loan to keep your business going. These are small *t* traumas.

Big *T* traumas are a by-product of exposure to horrific incidents of war, molestation as a child, or surviving a terrible car crash in which you or loved ones were significantly hurt. Big *T* traumas are life-altering events.

Everyone is different when it comes to the contents of their trauma reservoir in terms of how much they have endured and suffered, and their capacity to bear a burden of trauma. You have heard the idiom, "The straw that broke the camel's back," which alludes to a small event that causes a significant reaction because of the cumulative effects of other stressors.

There is a similar idiom, "The last drop makes the cup run over." Some of us have reservoirs close to full, and one last drop causes an overflow—or so it appears. In reality, it is the accumulation of all of the drops that causes a spillover.

Some of us are more fortunate and have plenty of room to manage emotional energy released from new traumatic events. The point is, you cannot judge how another person will react to adversity based on the characteristics of the situation. The core of psychology is the study of individual differences. Hence, the proverb, "Never judge another person until you've walked a mile in their shoes."

Once you have been injured, you will encounter professionals from various fields whose jobs are to make specialized judgments about your conditions, symptoms, and behaviors. Be open with them about how the stress of the accident has impacted you. Be transparent about your circumstances, your resources to cope, and the areas where you could use support. Clearly communicating (to the best of your ability) your issues and needs is essential to receiving the best supports.

SELF-LOVE

Nurture the capacity to be kind and empathic with yourself. You may use your injury recovery to learn to better cherish, value, and take care of yourself. Safeguarding your happiness is one of your most important responsibilities. If you are not fulfilled and satisfied with who you are, you are less likely to reach your full potential.

Henry Krystal repeatedly has said to me that the key to recovery from trauma comes from nurturing your capacity to experience pleasure. It is called the "emotional hedonic principle." When you have been traumatized, this critical self-care function can become compromised. Self-denial and self-sacrifice are often traits that can manifest and be a feature of depression and are sometimes related to emotions of shame and guilt.

Gabor Maté, author of *In the Realm of the Hungry Ghosts: Close Encounters with Addiction,* mentions that as a child, he learned to sacrifice "who he was" in order to have a relationship with his mother.[4] She was overwhelmed with the trauma of the Holocaust in Hungary, where he was born shortly after the Nazi invasion. Only as a mature man, after decades of self-sacrifice and dedicated work as a physician, did he realize how his mother's inability to cope with her trauma cast a lifelong shadow over him and his relationship with himself.

Krystal coined the term "survivor's guilt," which deals with the standard clinical observation that trauma survivors often experience unconscious guilt for having lived when others did not. It is an essential concept in trauma work that must always be considered when survivors are observed behaving in counterproductive, self-defeating, or self-destructive ways.

Many of my patients express that they feel guilty for or ashamed of their injuries and can be self-critical in their recovery progress. Share your feelings with a trusted loved one and your psychotherapist. It's important to take it a day at a time, celebrate your gains, however minor they may seem, and be gentle and kind with yourself.

I have patients do an exercise twice a day—look directly into their eyes in the mirror and say the words "I love you." This is not narcissism. It is a tool to develop compassion for oneself. Most of the problems of the world would instantly fall away if everyone loved themselves more. Self-love helps us to be compassionate, empathic, kind—and feel more connected to others.

The mirror exercise can be challenging in the beginning. However, put down this book for a moment, try it, and see what it does for you. Make it a habit. We receive a lot of societal messages that tell us to disapprove of ourselves unless we look or act a particular way. Learn to practice unconditional love for yourself. You are worthy of love simply because you exist. Practice by taking small steps and continue to nurture your capacity to express love for yourself.

PRACTICE FORGIVENESS

In trauma work, we often discover the need to forgive. But it is not the forgiveness of others that is most critical; it is forgiving yourself that is essential for your healing and recovery from some imagined flaw or mistake. Sometimes people deceive themselves with the false belief that they had control when, in fact, they were powerless. Or perhaps they did something that contributed to their own or someone else's injury. Examine yourself. Are there areas in your heart or your mind that require forgiveness? Some people need to self-forgive so they can become free from a self-imposed inner prison sentence. Forgiveness can open the door to enjoyment and a life worth living. Perhaps you blame yourself for your accident. Now is the time to forgive yourself, to move on, and to accept that everyone makes mistakes. Move forward from any guilt or self-blame and release any psychological shackles.

Dr. Martin Wunsch, a highly experienced and empathic psychotherapist, explained an exercise in which he teaches children how to take responsibility for their actions and how to forgive. He gives each child a jar of marbles, and every time they do something positive, they earn a marble to place in their jar. When they misbehave, a marble is taken from them. If they learn from their mistake, they receive three marbles back to add to their jars. The children who have made the most mistakes but have learned from them end up with the most marbles.

When I first became a psychotherapist, I was struck by the horrific events that have happened to so many people. I wondered just how they had coped with such overwhelming trauma. Decades of doing this work have shown me how resilient people are. When we are the victims of terrible events that result from other people's actions, we tend to blame ourselves on some level. I have always known that forgiveness is vital, but it took a long time for me to realize that the key that unlocks forgiveness is to a door within ourselves, as opposed to a door outside of ourselves. Again, I encourage you to look within and see if you need to let yourself off some mental hook you have been quietly torturing yourself with since your accident occurred.

Mistakes are essential for mental, spiritual, and emotional growth. We all make them. Take responsibility for your actions and consider giving yourself a pardon. You may be a righteous person, wrongly accused. If a drunk driver ran into your car while you were driving home, no, you do not *have* to forgive the drunk driver. You are entitled to your anger for their irresponsible behavior that harmed you. However, being chronically angry is not healthy, and will do nothing to the person who injured you. What *is* critical is understanding that you may need to forgive yourself for staying at your friend's house for an extra cup of coffee when your initial impulse was to leave 20 minutes earlier. You had no way of knowing your delayed departure would put you in the crosshairs of a drunk driver, for example. Forgiving the drunk driver for their transgression, too, may help you resolve some of your anger. It's not required, of course, but it can be another big step on the path toward healing.

If you were the drunk or distracted driver who caused the accident, you need to take responsibility for your actions, do your own forgiveness work, and correct the behavior that caused others so much pain and suffering. Look for ways to make positive contributions to other's lives.

Music acts as a wonderful healing conduit and aid to recovery. I love the song "Amazing Grace." Listen to the words and see if you can find yourself within them. It was written by someone who had previously taken part in an activity that caused great suffering to others and is perhaps the most well-known healing song ever written for trauma survivors.[5] Another song that can facilitate the grief process is "Fields of Gold" by Eva Cassidy.[6] I played this recording at my father's funeral. Cassidy's voice is beautiful and haunting—even more so given that she died of cancer at a young age just as she was rocketing to superstardom.

One of my teachers, Martin Prechtel, trained as a Mayan shaman in Guatemala. He has written several books about his experiences, including *Secrets of the Talking Jaguar.*[7] One of his duties as the village shaman was to learn the ancient songs that had the power to facilitate grieving. When someone in the village died, he would sing these songs to make everyone cry. According to Mayan belief, the tears of the grieving create a lake that allows the departed soul to travel on a boat to the next world. The tears are necessary for the soul's survival, and the shaman's job is to produce them. Without the tears, the soul is trapped in this world forever.

Returning again to my mentor, Henry Krystal, who often said, "Good therapy is good grieving," we must mourn the person we once were so that we can create our new self. Life is a process of letting go and creating anew. On and on the cycle continues, calling for periods of grieving. Krystal would also say that the capacity to grieve is a gift and a vital function. Some people have endured such great losses in life that their ability to grieve may have become compromised. Much support is needed in such cases. We must remember to celebrate and feel gratitude for new psychological growth as it happens.

When you have lost a loved one, the grief process continues in some form throughout your life. However, it will change over time. The saying "Time heals all wounds" bears truth. There is also a saying in the trauma field, "You will never forget, but when you have healed, you will not have to remember." It means that with time, the painful mental intrusions related to your trauma will begin to feel less intense and will not dominate your mind in the way they once did.

THE TRAUMA MEMBRANE

In my work with victims of catastrophic stress, I find psychoanalyst Jacob Lindy's concept of the trauma membrane extremely helpful.[8] The term "trauma membrane" refers to a kind of psychological protective sphere that a survivor creates around himself or herself following a catastrophic event. People around them will be emotionally shut out unless they feel an empathic attunement to the survivor's experience. Trauma-informed psychotherapy must be performed by an empathic therapist who can be permitted inside the psychological perimeter created by the survivor.

TIPS

- *Your recovery offers a great opportunity to hone your intuition.*
- *Look on YouTube for Louise Hay's recorded guided meditations on self-esteem and self-love and have a listen.[9] Louise is a trauma survivor who recovered and used her experience to benefit others through her motivational writings and the founding of an incredible self-help publishing dynasty.*
- *Create and listen to a special playlist of inspirational songs.*

9

THE BENEFITS OF PSYCHOTHERAPY

The conflict between the will to deny horrible events and the will to proclaim them aloud is the central dialectic of psychological trauma.

—Judith Lewis Herman[1]

Vulnerability is the birthplace of innovation, creativity, and change.

—Brene Brown[2]

We are an overmedicated and unheard society.

—Dr. Jill Stocker[3]

WHAT PSYCHOTHERAPY CAN OFFER

As an intern, I practiced psychotherapy in an outpatient mental health clinic in Columbus, Ohio. Since then, and many thousands of psychotherapy sessions later, I have heard countless patients say that without psychotherapy they would not have survived the emotional challenges presented by the traumatic incidences in their lives. Many confided that the surgeries to repair their damaged spines were essential to their recovery, but that undergoing psychotherapy was vital in reclaiming their lives.

Find the most experienced psychotherapist who focuses on trauma and, if possible, is experienced with working with car-accident survivors. A specialist will guide you through the psychological recovery process in your overall rehabilitation.

In the past, psychotherapy had a negative stigma associated with it, but that has since dissipated. When struggling with the loss, tragedy, and confusions life has thrown at you, getting help when your inner resources are exhausted shows a significant sign of strength.

Anxiety and depression are common symptoms associated with the auto-crash experience. Sometimes panic attacks, cognitive problems from head trauma, or a combination of factors such as sleep disturbance, anxiety, and medication side effects make driving impossible and day-to-day tasks difficult, if not completely overwhelming.

While there are many kinds of psychotherapists with various professional training and perspectives, research has shown that regardless of the "school" of psychotherapy, it is the relationship between psychotherapist and patient that counts the most. Effective psychotherapy considers the person as a whole and notes how the trauma impacts all aspects of functioning.

Intensive individual psychotherapy, once or twice a week, can offer the support needed while you undergo medical tests, evaluations, and procedures necessary for understanding the extent of your injuries, your personal response to treatment, and all of your unfolding needs and challenges. This thorough clinical contact helps identify ongoing problems that might otherwise be missed. The data can be shared with the other members of your medical team through clinical reports. Appropriate professional referrals are made as new problems are identified. You, as a "whole," must be considered, as many aspects of your injuries need to be addressed by different specialists.

When someone has survived a devastating car accident, the type of psychotherapy required is different from what the "worried-well" need when attempting to navigate life's challenges. Support, trauma-recovery work, ongoing evaluation, and interdisciplinary cooperation all play a role in giving you the best rehabilitation outcome.

Involve key family members who support your recovery in the psychotherapy sessions. With information and insights, your family can reduce the ripple effects from your injuries. Ideally, involving the entire family unit should be standard protocol, but this is not always a viable option.

Because documentation of your conditions, symptoms, and response to treatment is so critical, make certain your psychotherapist understands the medicolegal dimensions of your situation and is comfortable providing high-quality reports. Insurance professionals read these reports to determine if they will pay for your ongoing psychological care.

Your psychological records will also be examined by legal professionals, and your psychotherapist may need to provide reports to the courts. In this sense, the psychotherapist becomes a forensic psychotherapist who gives opinions regarding causation and prognosis. In the academic world, these different dimensions would be kept separate—and sometimes they are—by employing expert witnesses. But in the real world, these roles are mostly combined.

Be careful who you share your traumatic experience with. Many people will not understand, and you may risk further psychological injury. Sadly, insurance firms send many auto-accident trauma survivors to one of their company's mental health practitioners where they are sometimes treated with a lack of respect and empathy and are even met with psychological abuse. Or, they may be treated empathetically but then betrayed in a written report, which wounds clients emotionally and sometimes financially. For example, the mental health practitioner blames all of the survivor's current difficulties on traumatic events that happened *before* the accident and discounts the impact of their serious car-crash injuries. I have unfortunately seen examiners who have never written a helpful report for a trauma survivor.

As in all relationships, communication is essential, so ask tons of questions and gain as much information as possible. With traumatic injuries, psychotherapy needs to be more interactive due to all of the moving parts that are in operation. Not all psychotherapists are comfortable dealing with the legal dimension of auto trauma, so be confident that yours has the forensic background to cope with sub-poenas, records requests, attorneys, and the courts.

MEDITATION AND GUIDED IMAGERY

Meditation

I recommend meditation as an essential tool for life.

As an undergraduate student studying psychology at Ohio State, I realized the necessity of learning to better manage my anxiety. The endless progression of tests and examinations that lay ahead felt overwhelming, on top of the stress of other everyday developmental and relational challenges confronting me as a late adolescent.

One of the blessings that befell me was a pamphlet announcing an informational meeting on the benefits of Transcendental Medita-tion. Looking back over the decades, it was perhaps one of the most important, positive decisions I have made thus far in my life. I signed up for the course and scraped together the several hundreds of dollars needed to pay the tuition, which was not an easy thing to do at that time.

I began to practice Transcendental Meditation (TM), and my friends quickly commented that I seemed different. Indeed, I felt like a changed man. This technique invited calmness to come over my mind. As a high-achieving and chronically anxious adolescent, I had never experienced this sensation before. Through TM, I learned how to access a peaceful sanctuary in my mind. For 20 minutes twice a day, or more if necessary, I enjoyed the respite. As a result of my meditation practice, my studies became easier, my memory improved, and I was more present as a human being. I continue to meditate to this day.

Access to formal meditation training is still limited in the United States. If possible, take the meditation course offered at a Transcen-dental Meditation facility. Maharishi Mahesh Yogi (Maharishi means "great seer"), an Indian guru, founded TM. He taught thousands as he traveled the world. In the late 1960s, he became a guru to the Beatles, which inspired them to incorporate elements of TM in their music.

If you do not have in-person access to a professional meditation trainer, you can google "how to meditate" and hear a short explanation from Transcendental Meditation on a few easy steps to learn. On Transcendental Meditation's website, the technique is described as an effortless way to recharge your mind and body and create a positive state of being. I would add that experiencing the meditative state also disengages our fear response of fight/flight/freeze hardwired for our species' survival.

Several years ago, I attended one of the first continuing education courses on meditation and guided imagery, offered by Harvard Medical School. The instructor was Daniel P. Brown, a Harvard psychology professor, highly experienced meditator, and student/master of meditation. He explained that while meditation has been practiced for thousands of years in the East, it has only recently been embraced in the West. Westerners often have a different meditation objective to Easterners.

In the East, the reason for practicing meditation is to achieve enlightenment or oneness with the divine. In the West, particularly as embraced by complementary and alternative medicine, the primary goal is stress reduction.

Herbert Benson, a cardiologist and Harvard Medical School professor, is one of the pioneers in stress management. Benson broke new ground in the 1970s by studying the health benefits of meditation, which he describes in his self-help book, *The Relaxation Response*.[4] His book became the number one book recommended by clinical psychologists for managing stress. He went on to found the Benson-Henry Institute for Mind Body Medicine at Massachusetts General Hospital, which continues to do research and educate professionals on the global health benefits of mind-body medicine.

I attended the institute's continuing education course and heard Benson talk about the resistance he first encountered by the medical community when he began his research. As a young cardiologist, Benson was told by his colleagues that he would ruin his career by studying meditation, and that he should just stick to mainstream cardiology. But he could not ignore the word "tension" in the word "hypertension" and believed it was essential to relieve it. This is precisely what meditation promises to achieve. Heart disease is still considered the number one cause of death in the United States.

Interestingly, Benson's Harvard laboratory was the same one used by Walter Cannon. Cannon was a Harvard professor of physiology who discovered the fight-or-flight response, also known as the acute stress response. He studied the "stress hormones" of epinephrine (adrenaline) and norepinephrine that are mediated by the sympathetic nervous system. These stress hormones play an active role in response to vehicular trauma.

Benson's work was based on the concept of homeostasis developed by the French physiologist Claude Bernard. *Homeostasis* refers to the concept of how cells maintain stability and balance while interacting with a complex, interconnected physiological milieu. Meditation has been shown to support this stability and equilibrium on a mind-body level.

When asked the difference between a psychologist and a psychiatrist, I often give the somewhat flip answer, "Psychiatrists prescribe medication, and psychologists prescribe meditation."

Guided Imagery

Guided imagery has been just as vital to my practice as meditation. In chapter 6, I introduced you to Belleruth Naparstek and her fantastic guided imagery books and trainings.

The first sample I heard of Naparstek's guided imagery addressed trauma recovery. Her guided imagery amazed me with its power to induce an altered state similar to what I had enjoyed experiencing with TM. I now routinely use her guided imagery with many of my trauma patients to teach them how to disengage from their anxiety states and experience mental calmness along with deep relaxation, without having to rely on alcohol or drugs. The technique helps them to better cope with emotional distress.

When I asked Naparstek what she attributed her phenomenal success in life to, she thought for a moment, smiled, and said her husband calls her a "chronically delusional optimist." Of everything I have learned in the field of mental health, Naparstek's guided imagery tools have been the most practical.

IT HELPS TO TALK

While recovering from your auto crash, you may fear that you will never improve nor have the abilities, capabilities, and qualities you had before you were injured. Most likely, you are frustrated that your recovery is taking so long and you're anxious about the medical uncertainties. Fears cast big shadows when kept inside. By talking through your worries and concerns with a psychotherapist who understands what's involved with postaccident trauma, you will feel more empowered and less alone.

Sharing your thoughts and feelings with someone who will not judge you and who can metaphorically hold your pain can offer the relief you need. The ability to step back and gain a fresh perspective on your challenges and identify resources through therapy is crucial to successfully navigating your recovery. Unfortunately, I have seen many people struggle when they stubbornly insist they can do it alone. Psychotherapy is an investment in yourself that pays big dividends and prevents further difficulties for you and your loved ones.

TIPS

- *Before your psychotherapy session, it can help to write down any specific issues you want to address.*
- *Talk to your attorney prior to going to an Independent Medical Evaluation and ask what you are advised to do if an examiner becomes abusive. You are there in good faith to be examined for your car-accident-related injuries. You are not there to endure*

abuse. You have the power to terminate an examination. Document the abusive actions of the examiner and notify your attorney and your insurance carrier.

- *There are many different meditation techniques. Explore and find a practice that works best for you.*

10

GROUP PSYCHOTHERAPY—YOU ARE NOT ALONE

The best part of being in a group is that you don't have to do everything alone.

—Anonymous

We don't heal in isolation, but in community.

—S. Kelley Harrell[1]

THE EXPERIENCE OF GROUP PSYCHOTHERAPY

You may have heard of self-help support groups such as AA. There are also many structured and facilitated support groups for navigating the postaccident world that you might find helpful, including group psychotherapy. The benefits of group psychotherapy are numerous. Most important, group therapy really helps you to realize that you are not alone. It provides a safe environment to share your struggles with people who offer emotional support and truly understand what you're going through.

I have conducted a psychotherapy group for car-accident survivors for the past 12 years. We meet three times a week for one-hour sessions. Group members also come for individual psychotherapy

usually once per week. The focus is on recovering from the psychological and physical trauma caused by their injuries: dealing with
PTSD, TBI, pain, and all the related family, job, future, and litigation stressors.

Convincing a new patient to come to group for the first time is
often tricky. Sometimes, I have to repeatedly discuss the benefits for
many months before they agree to give it a try. After their first
session, they regret not having attended sooner.

While doing my postdoctoral residency in a community hospital
psychiatry program, I conducted three group sessions a day, five
days a week, and consistently observed its effectiveness in helping
trauma survivors connect with others. One of the greatest dangers of
trauma relates to the tendency to isolate and withdraw from other
people. Seclusion cuts you off from family, friends, and life. Group
is the perfect milieu to restore the vital energy that trauma sometimes robs you of.

The power of group therapy is that it can accomplish, in a short
while, what can take much longer to accomplish in individual
psychotherapy. As they say, two heads are better than one, and
sometimes six, seven, or eight are better still in unraveling the devastating impact of trauma. Also, group therapy offers the opportunity to learn new ways to find the will to go on, which post-traumatic depression often saps.

When a new member joins the group, we introduce the rules,
expectations, and the other members. Creating an atmosphere of
safety and trust is fundamental. Everyone agrees to strict and total
confidentiality about who attends the group and what is said. It
forbids outside relationships between group members and insists on
maintaining healthy therapeutic boundaries. Noncritical, nonjudg-
mental attitudes are expected in the group interactions. Everyone
pledges that what happens in group, stays in group.

We use a "talking stick" donated by a member whose Native
American great-great-grandfather handed down to him. When you
have the talking stick, other members give you the floor, and there
can be no interruptions, unless invited to speak. It also gives members something to do with their hands while they talk. There can be

a lot of nervous energy, and the ancient stick provides a structure that serves to ground everyone.

The healing experiences from group are difficult to mass-produce in "evidence-based" manuals that have hijacked the art and soul of psychotherapy. Not that I have anything against evidence; it is critical to advancing the field of psychology. However, some of the real guts of what makes it worth it for a psychotherapist to get up in the morning are sadly lacking when statisticians run the show. Effective psychotherapy shares many elements of the shamanic healers who have supported the health of the human species since the dawn of time—before there were statisticians and insurance adjusters. What's significant in terms of coping with life's challenges can be difficult to quantify in a psychological test score. The results of psychotherapy cannot be easily measured.

Traumatic-brain-injury survivors, who often have communication challenges due to cognitive and speech difficulties, find group particularly helpful. Common problems related to post-traumatic brain injuries are word-finding difficulties, comprehension, stuttering and stammering, and distractibility. TBI patients find a safe environment to practice speaking in a group situation where they know they are understood and supported, which is priceless for their growth and recovery.

I have a co-therapist trained in drama therapy visit our group on a weekly basis to support therapeutic work on a deeper level. She determines a common theme that emerges from the members' check-ins. She then works with the most energetic issue from an expressive therapy perspective. For example, in a recent session, members shared one word from their check-ins to describe their prevailing emotional experiences. The following words most described how group members dealt with their traumas that day: running on empty, depleted, overwhelmed, challenged, physically and mentally fatigued, depressed, and distracted.

My co-therapist shared that, as she was rushing to get to the group, she noticed her gas tank was on empty. She faced the dilemma of stopping to get gas and being late or chancing it and getting to group on time. The tension she experienced from this anxiety-provoking situation inspired her to use it as a therapeutic tool that served to open the shared experience of others. Everyone in the group identified with the experience of emotionally running on empty.

She then worked with the theme we identified as "running on empty." We probed to discover what would make everyone feel less depleted; what would "fill their tanks"? Group members identified resources that worked for them. For some, it was taking a walk with a family member or friend, or spending time with a grandchild or a beloved pet. It could also be a nap, a massage, or eating a nice meal with a loved one.

Participating in the therapeutic group interactions and benefiting from the dynamics created a high-octane attitude for the coming weekend. One member said he needed his Vitamin G (*G* for group). There is something primordial about a group's power. After all, as a human species, we have survived by forming groups.

RESOURCE DEVELOPMENT AND INSTALLATION TECHNIQUE (RDI)

The gas tank exercise is similar to a technique called Resource Development and Installation (RDI) named by EMDR (Eye Movement Desensitization and Reprocessing) advocate Andrew M. Leeds, PhD. Emotional strength is imagined and "installed" psychologically during the session. A skill, trait, or quality to be "installed" could be assertiveness, a self-care action, or an attitude of self-compassion. The technique is focused on empowering oneself as well as receiving empowerment from others, which is modeled and supported consistently in group psychotherapy. A creative process, group interaction benefits cannot be learned from a manual; they must be experienced.

TRANSPERSONAL DRAMA THERAPY

In 2019, I participated in a four-day psychodrama group training led by Saphira Linden, creator of Transpersonal Drama Therapy—one of the most influential courses I've ever attended. The training was held in Linden's ancient theater in a suburb of Boston. The participants were professional actors and drama therapists in training.

Linden is a creative master at helping people delve deep into the psyche and identify those places where trauma continues to operate and drain life force energy. The experience is transformative. All "manualized therapists" should be required to participate in such training. Having the experience of doing therapeutic work on themselves, therapists would be more effective in helping others.

GROUP THERAPY CASE EXAMPLE: JEFF

Jeff became disabled from severe neck and back injuries as a result of a high-speed, multicar pileup several years ago. Depression, anxiety, and pain began to tear him down, and he felt that he could not go on.

"Thank the good Lord for group therapy. I never even knew it existed before my accident," Jeff said. "One of my doctors suggested I attend, but I was super resistant. I didn't want other people to know what kind of darkness lurked beneath my mask.

"I had the wrong impression about group therapy. I thought people just whined about this or that hurting. What I quickly learned was that group takes you beyond the pain to a greater appreciation of how things are when you get injured. You learn about the things you can do that help you not only survive, but also thrive again.

"I had cracked five vertebrae in my neck. My doctor told me this injury meant the end of my career. I felt lost. Nobody understood the kind of pain I endured. At my first group therapy visit, I met people who inspired me. In one visit, I knew I needed this group interaction in my life.

"During a session, you tell it like it is: how your family is responding, your wife, your brother, your children. You speak to those who comprehend your situation, who are supportive, and who can find new ways to manage it."

Jeff sighed deeply, "You get tired of explaining to people who don't understand the depth of what happened to you. You show your scars as you try to convince people that you have injuries that aren't going to fix themselves. My friends and family couldn't fathom how catastrophic my injuries were. After my first couple of doctor visits, I knew that I would never be the same. A guy that got up every morning at 4 a.m., I had my own business and worked hard to grow it. I intended on continuing this until my 70s. The crash took that plan from me. I had to make a new life, and that was not easy.

"The first time Dr. Zender brought up group therapy, I was scared. I worried about explaining my injuries because I thought my words could get back to an insurance person and be used against me. Or, maybe a group member had the same doctor and would say something that I didn't want that doctor to hear. In our group, everything is confidential. That made a significant difference for me because I could pretty much say what was on my mind, reveal my pain level and what my injuries were, and discuss the frustration of dealing with family members, doctors, lawyers, and insurance hassles.

"Group is a haven because the listeners are going through similar problems. By helping these people, by sharing your experience, it helps your emotions get back on track. You are given the opportunity to share people's psychological issues, which are as damaging as physical problems. In the process, you gain a new perspective of your own challenges. It warms your heart to see how others respond to support and understanding when they are dealing with devastating injuries and situations that overwhelm them.

"I don't know if I would have survived without the group's support. Admitting your emotions helps you get some distance so you can calmly approach situations. Group brings me inner peace.

"Getting hurt isolates a person. It can leave you feeling alone, afraid, in the dark night of the soul. After a group session, I feel much better because I get answers to something I didn't understand. My concerns are addressed, and my worrying relieved. And, even better, I provide that for someone else.

"My advice? If you have been severely injured and have a long recovery ahead of you, find a group. It is the best thing that could happen to you because you can say and show what you're feeling, and somebody going through the same thing can help you find solace. Or you can help someone else find it. It is such a great feeling to give in that way.

"Since my accident, dealing with the pain alone has been crazy. A lot of people are against medication so that's another thing about the group. Maybe you don't want to do pain medication, and you don't have to do medication to get relief because when you come out of the meeting after just talking about it, it makes you feel so much better. Maybe you don't need pain medication for the rest of the day. It helps me find ways of coping with pain without turning to medication.

"Does my physical pain level go up when I'm depressed? Yes. No doubt about that. When your mood is down, and you blame others, feel frustrated, or hold on to anger, this translates into tension and increased physical pain. When you feel like a victim, that's no place to stay. There are so many challenges we share. We pull through things that you wouldn't believe—physically, mentally, and sexually—you got a ton of issues to deal with when you are catastrophically injured. You can bring that out in group, so it doesn't register as more physical pain from the feelings you've tried to stuff down.

"The accident left me disabled. My relationships with friends changed. Those I thought were friends weren't. I was lost. I never thought I'd find another person who could empathize with my mood changes, my depression, and my rage. It was a frightening time. In group, you have a place to go where everybody is the same and going through similar stuff.

"It's helpful to explain to each other how sexually, mentally, and physically, we can't do the things that we used to do before our accidents. But you realize you can get around all that because somebody in that group is going through the same thing. Maybe they found a tool for coping you didn't know about. You can try it. It could work for you as well.

"I needed help with one of my major issues. Anger. I couldn't let go of the fact that I'd no longer have the career I had spent a lifetime creating. Someone's carelessness took that from me. I couldn't have the same lifestyle I had, couldn't provide for my family the way I used to. Going from working 16 hours a day running a successful business to having to live on Social Security benefits is not an easy transition. That's a bitter pill to swallow. By seeing others deal with the same losses and watching them find ways of going on, I was able to pull back from my situation.

"Speaking my mind and letting out the rage and the rest of the demons help my healing process. You can't hold that stuff in. If you don't exorcise the darkness, it will eat you up. We need to find new paths in life now that the old ones are closed. We can't do that alone."

TIPS

- *Find a psychotherapy group in your area through your case manager, healthcare providers, or a search on the internet. There are also support groups available online.*
- *If you feel overwhelmed by therapies and doctor visits, make sure you allocate some time for enjoyable preaccident activities that you are still able to do.*
- *If you have an iPhone, both the iCal and Notes features can be useful to keep track of your thoughts, feelings, reminders, and appointments.*

11

KEY PROFESSIONALS WHO CAN HELP

A short pencil is better than a long memory.

—Unknown

After a car crash has left you seriously injured, summon "all the king's horses and all the king's men" to get yourself put back together again. We are fortunate to have vast resources that address every aspect of the arduous rehabilitation process. Recovery might be longer than expected, so save time by putting the right people in place from the start. Do your research. Find top practitioners in your area who are dedicated to patient advocacy. First, they must be promoters of the truth, and second, they need to support you and your path to healing. This chapter identifies key professionals, outside of a psychotherapist, who can assist you.

CASE MANAGERS

If you require services from multiple specialists, get a case manager you feel comfortable with. Be sure they will enthusiastically and diligently work on your behalf. Case managers hold degrees and certifications such as CBIS (certified brain injury specialist) or CCM (Certified Case Manager). Their academic and professional training can be from different fields that include nursing, social work, and mental health.

The Commission for Case Manager Certification (CCMC) in the United States states that case managers have several job responsibilities: ensuring appropriate care, educating and empowering, coordinating care, aiding in identifying issues, creating goals, and helping clients move from one care setting to the next.[1] Under CCMC's core principles, a board-certified case manager places the patient's interests above their own. This is critical. Be confident that you trust your case manager and are sure he/she will be in your corner.

Interview case managers before choosing one. Clarify expectations and have a written contract so you know what to expect from them. Do you want them with you at your medical appointments, or assisting with necessary paperwork that might overwhelm you, or facilitating communication among your other providers?

One of the biggest problems I've encountered with case managers is that they do not return calls promptly. This also is the case with some attorneys. Clearly understand the expectations regarding communication and the best ways to keep it optimal. Ask whether it's best to text, e-mail, or call. If you send something by e-mail, see if you can also text to confirm they received it. If there is any urgency, texting seems to have become the preferred way to communicate.

An excellent case manager is invaluable when they facilitate your rehabilitation process. If your case manager is not performing the agreed-upon duties, move on. Be sure you choose a practitioner with an outstanding reputation for providing high-quality, reliable services.

PM&R (PHYSIATRIST) PHYSICIANS

Physiatrists, also called PM&Rs (Physical Medicine and Rehabilitation specialists), are physicians who specialize in rehabilitative medicine. These doctors possess either an MD or DO degree and operate as your "quarterback" when you "move down the field" toward recovery. Specific procedures and protocols must be followed to receive services and have the costs covered by your insurance carrier. The PM&R doctor knows the insurance process, what kinds of documentation are needed, and which treatments and evaluations you will require based upon your injuries and symptoms. They often provide pain management and perform minimally invasive surgeries.

Find a PM&R who is known for their competence and patient advocacy. I receive many referrals from PM&R physicians who understand the importance of a provider who addresses the psychological side of trauma.

If you have chosen an excellent case manager and PM&R, they should have a network of relevant specialists and know the top practitioners for necessary evaluations and treatment. Or perhaps your point of entry to the healthcare system postaccident was through someone who was already treating you. Maybe you were seeing a psychologist, chiropractor, or primary care physician before the crash happened.

Regardless, an entire team is required in *polytrauma* cases. You were exposed to forces that may have affected every organ system of your body including your brain, eyes, ears, muscles, nerves, ligaments, tendons, heart, lungs, bladder, and glands. It can take a long time for symptoms to appear. When they do, you'll need the right specialist to address whatever problem develops.

COGNITIVE REHABILITATION SPECIALISTS

If you have a TBI, specialized speech and occupational therapists may be critical for you to reach your maximum level of rehabilitation. Based upon psychological and neuropsychological evaluation findings or clinical assessment by your PM&R physician, neurologist, or neuropsychologist, it could be determined that you would benefit from these services. Some countries have specialized brain injury clinics with teams of trained neurorehab specialists. If available, take advantage. Help find compensatory strategies for dealing with your cognitive challenges. Some clinics are community based, which means the therapists will come to your home once, twice, or three times a week. Your situation will determine if in-home or center-based treatment will work best for you.

ATTORNEYS

It is essential to vet attorneys. A former attorney general of the United States said that 85 percent of attorneys do harm to their clients. You want to find a top-tier lawyer, one of the 5 percent with an outstanding reputation for integrity, competence, and honesty. And be confident that he/she is an expert in auto law (and brain trauma if you have a TBI).

DEALING WITH HEALTHCARE PROVIDERS

My patients sometimes complain that physicians don't listen. The five-minute appointment with their neurologist (after sitting for two hours in a busy waiting room) isn't enough time to address all of their symptoms and difficulties—for example, the 100 trillion neural connections in their brain not working properly since a rollover car crash.

Or the five-minute psychiatry appointment, "How are your medications working, any problems? The front desk will have your refill prescriptions, and I'll see you in three months." It seems that many psychiatry practices could operate as fast-food establishments. Pull up to the speaker and the psychiatrist asks, "How are the meds working? Pull up to the next window for your refills." To me, this is pure insanity.

One of the great ills of our society is "managed" medical care standards that dictate a healthcare appointment should be 10 or 15 minutes. Finding professionals who actually listen to you, ask relevant questions, and speak to you by addressing your concerns may be difficult, but it's worth the effort. You are not bound to see one professional or another and you should only pay for services that are working for you.

Cutting someone loose who does not fulfill your needs is okay. Interview new doctors, therapists, or other helping professionals before committing to them as a patient. Great healthcare providers that can give you the time that you require are out there! Don't give up if the first or second or third cannot provide what you need.

A NOTE FOR HEALTHCARE PROVIDERS

During one of Dr. Herbert Benson's courses I attended on mind-body medicine at Harvard, an internal medicine physician shared his practice of finding out a patient's hobbies and allowing them time to talk about it. This information often proved essential for diagnostics and let the doctor have a brief mental respite from the stress of his work to imagine what it would feel like to be fly-fishing in Montana or sailing on the ocean. It was a technique that made the sometimes-crushing stress of clinical work tolerable, protected the doctor from burnout, and increased his job satisfaction. As a healthcare provider, it is vital that you ensure you take good care of your own physical and mental health.

TIPS

- *No one professional that aids you in your recovery has all of the answers. It's a team effort, and you are the leader. Remember to ask for what you need.*
- *Ask a family member or friend to help you keep an organized file of all of your medical documentation.*
- *Enlist the help of family and friends for finding a good attorney and ask for assistance with getting to and from appointments if needed.*

12

HOW TO DEAL WITH YOUR INSURANCE COMPANY

The world has enough for everyone's needs, but not everyone's greed.

—Mahatma Gandhi[1]

A culture that denies its natural empathy is dehumanized.

—Joseph Tafur, MD[2]

YES! YOU NEED A LAWYER

You must face the fact that surviving a collision and being injured now represents a medicolegal financial challenge to your insurance carrier that you must defend in court. I once heard a seasoned insurance defense lawyer say, "You *must* have an attorney if you are injured in an auto accident." I respected him for saying this since his job was to represent the interests of insurance companies.

Stress related to dealing with your insurance company could fill several books. Most people have no idea how distressing and perplexing the insurance side is.

Did you know your insurance company could require you to see doctors that *they* pay to evaluate your condition? These doctors perform what's called an independent medical examination or IME. As the insurance company pays for the doctor's time, the issue of the doctor actually being "independent" is questionable.

Some doctors who perform these evaluations earn most of their income from this work. These doctors form close relationships with the IME agencies that hire them. Plaintiff attorneys prefer the term defense medical evaluation (DME) because often the doctor works to protect the insurance company from having to pay benefits to the injured claimant. True, there are fraudulent patients, which the insurance companies use as justification for demanding IMEs or DMEs. However, these exams are frequently skewed in favor of the insurance company and result in legitimately injured claimants being prevented from receiving the care they need to recover.

PAIN, SOFT TISSUE INJURIES, AND INSURANCE COMPANIES

Jay M. Feinman is a distinguished professor of law at Rutgers University. In his highly researched and revealing book, *Delay, Deny, Defend*, he says, "Claims are handled well when insurance companies pay what they owe, promptly and without muss or fuss."[3] When soft tissue injuries are involved, insurance claim handling is often not done well. For clinicians and attorneys working with car-accident patients and insurance companies, Feinman's book is *the* Bible.

Feinman writes that, as late as the 1970s, the insurance industry standard was to settle claims fairly and not to chisel the public. In the past, claims adjusters had considerable discretion in settling claims impartially, and they received extensive medical training to perform their jobs well.

Currently, insurance adjusters have fewer options and receive little training. I recently spoke with a retired senior insurance adjuster who had worked for one of the major United States insurance companies for more than 30 years. She confirmed this shift in the industry and said that new adjusters often receive little or no training before handling medical claims that dramatically affect the lives of the insured. While there are still some excellent "claim representatives," as they are now frequently called, because of the insurance companies'concerns for their companies' profits, there clearly has been a move away from providing fair care to injured policyholders.

Professor Feinman indicates that the insurance industry frequently uses a technology information system called Colossus. Colossus compiles and analyzes all of the information available on an injury claim and spits out a dollar value. According to Feinman, this technology favors efficiency and profits over accuracy and fairness.

Under a management model first introduced to the insurance industry by consulting firm McKinsey & Company, adjusters' performance evaluations were tied to the company's business needs. According to Feinman, in the McKinsey doctrine of profits above fairness, crashes that resulted in less than broken bones or immediately apparent injuries were to be considered "subjective" injuries and given the acronym designation "MIST" (minor impact, soft tissue) cases. This was part of a business approach to cases called "segmentation" of claims. Claims were put into different categories, analyzed, and treated in a manner to reduce payouts, deny payments, and trigger litigation—all done with the ultimate objective of increasing profits. The McKinsey model included various strategies to dissuade injured policyholders from hiring an attorney. Insurance companies now operate according to the McKinsey model, although many may deny that fact.

If you have been in a collision, you *must* seek competent legal counsel. Find the best personal injury attorney and follow their advice. You and your family's future may entirely depend on it. Not all attorneys are created equally, so do your homework before you choose one to represent your interests.

THE CRIMINALIZATION OF SURVIVAL

Surveillance

The *Oxford New Desk Dictionary and Thesaurus* defines the noun "surveillance" as "close observation, especially of a suspected person."[4]

Are *you* a suspect in need of surveillance? A criminal? If you have been injured in a car crash, it may feel as though your insurance company thinks so. And if they do, prepare for professional surveillance by their investigators. Your crime? Surviving an accident that resulted in serious injuries and some level of disability. The world of insurance surveillance smacks of the attempted criminalization of survival, but it may, in fact, be your best friend—if you're truthful about your injuries.

You may be shocked to learn that insurance companies frequently hire specialized investigators to follow and photograph you hoping to find you doing something you say you cannot do because of your injuries. Because fraud is a legitimate threat to insurance companies, they sometimes take extreme measures to investigate. It is legal for them to videotape and photograph your every move as they attempt to invalidate your claims of severe injury. If investigators capture images of you doing an activity you've said you cannot do because of your injuries, your entire claim can be dismissed. It is even possible for you to be prosecuted for committing fraud.

The level of surveillance varies according to what you report about your injuries and the business model of your insurance company. Frequently, there is a stakeout in your neighborhood—near your house or anywhere a telescoping camera lens can focus on you. In psychological injury claims, tight face shots are preferred; if you are smiling and laughing, your claim of overwhelming (chronic) depression can be countered, despite solid medical evidence. All that matters is how the pictures are perceived in the courtroom.

Sometimes, an investigator will be a few feet away from you while you shop. Let's say, you bend as you try on a pair of shoes. If you've claimed you cannot dress yourself, the evidence will damage your case. It may not matter that bending caused severe pain and that you overextended yourself as you tried on the shoes. Pictures or videos created by investigators can be detrimental, and the insurance company will use whatever ammunition they can to destroy your credibility.

The catch is that sometimes you may do things you should not be doing—like lifting a baby when your doctor has given you a weight restriction. Yes, this action causes more pain and risks further injury, but at that moment, you're willing to pay the price. Just know that you may have to justify that activity to your legal team and possibly in court.

A brain injury can cause judgment impairment. You may not remember that your doctor told you not to bend or twist. Or you may suffer impulsivity and act on desires and urges without consideration of their consequences. The judge and jury will have to decide the merits of your case and reach their own conclusions. Be aware, however, that your case can settle out of court through negotiations between your attorney and the defense lawyers representing the insurance company.

Insurance investigators also stalk social media and pull images of you that they hope will besmirch your character or integrity if your case does end up in front of a jury. Some unethical investigators will use pictures of you before the accident and present them to your doctors as if they were after the crash. When involved in litigation, social media can become a *real* pain because an insurance company can and will use posted information against you.

My knowledge of insurance surveillance is not just hearsay from my patients. Insurance companies sometimes ask me to review surveillance videos to challenge a patient's believability or for my opinions as to the severity of the reported injury.

One of the downfalls of the current legal system is that it sometimes punishes people for attempting to be more functional when a case is in litigation. When undergoing legal depositions and defense medical examinations, you can be made to feel as if you are facing the Spanish Inquisition—like damned if you do, or damned if you don't. But remember, if you have accurately presented your injuries and the disabilities they have caused, the insurance company's investigative approach should work to your benefit and support a fair settlement of your claim. When the investigative and surveillance approach is insensitive to the severity of your injuries and is handled in what Bill Kizorek, an international authority on the subject of video surveillance, refers to as in "an inflammatory or provocative manner," an expectation of human decency is breeched and can constitute secondary victimization.[5] Nevertheless, investigative monitoring does, for most people, feel like adding an insult to injury.

Being stalked can be extremely distressing but simply must be accepted as a fact of life in your post-injury recovery world. Just stay focused on your recovery and ensure that all of your doctor and therapy visits are well documented.

Important: Do not lie about or exaggerate your injuries. Insurance is there to take care of the injured, not to line the pockets of scammers. If you are truthful, you will receive care. However, the help of a skilled attorney can assist you with fighting any less than good faith handling by your insurance carrier.

CASE STUDY—MICHIGAN INSURANCE LAW

We recently witnessed the power of the insurance industry to impact society here in Michigan. After many years of intense lobbying, the insurance industry has succeeded in dismantling Michigan's model personal injury protection system in which people are covered *for life* and without monetary caps for medical and rehabilitation costs for any injuries or conditions that result from a crash. The 1973 Michigan law defined what was covered and required the insurance company to pay "all reasonable charges incurred for all reasonably necessary products, services, and accommodations for an injured person's care, recovery or rehabilitation."[6]

The enlightened law had not only allowed Michigan residents injured in auto collisions to obtain the best and most comprehensive care in the country but also prevented the costs of care associated with auto-collision injuries from being passed on to state and federal government insurance programs.

Starting in 2020, Michigan residents will have to choose if they want lifetime protection and will be forced to select coordinated medical coverage. This means that their health insurance will be billed as the primary insurance, and the fees of healthcare providers will be set by the insurance industry. Already, many of Michigan's premier medical facilities that treat people injured in auto crashes have announced that they will be closing their doors or scaling back services due to the severe limits imposed by the new law.

Michigan's 2020 insurance law is just another unfortunate example of the seemingly boundless power of the insurance industry to determine the fates and futures of countless lives. Perhaps as we look to the future, knowledgeable advocates, policy makers, and consumers of insurance products can find a way to work together to positively influence insurance laws and policies.

TIPS

- *Always read through and understand the coverage in your insurance policy. Ask for help if needed.*
- *Documentation is key for both your lawyers and insurance company. Get the most precise scans of your injuries possible. For example, MRIs can often show injury or damage that CTs and X-rays can't.*
- *If your injuries result in litigation, be wary of what you post online. Change your name on your accounts or consider closing your social media until after the smoke has cleared.*

13

CARING FOR YOUR INJURED LOVED ONE

People say that what we're all seeking is a meaning for life. I don't think that's what we're really seeking. I think that what we're seeking is an experience of being alive, so that our life experiences on the purely physical plane will have resonances with our own innermost being and reality, so that we actually feel the rapture of being alive.

—Joseph Campbell[1]

The emotional, medicolegal, and financial challenges that result from your loved one's injuries can put excessive stress and strain on your relationship. Marriages can be tested to the breaking point, relationships may dissolve, and the injured person's children may be confused and upset.

It may be difficult for you to understand what your loved one is going through and what is now expected from you. It can be overwhelming. Communication is key. If your loved one has a TBI, communication can be particularly challenging. Their emotions may be all over the place with outbursts of anger, frustration, and expressions of sadness and fear. You may notice personality changes, and it may be difficult to recognize the person you once knew. Remember that their planning and judgment may be impaired and they may not always know what's best for them. It's important to have patience with the recovery process and know that, over time, there will be improvements. Most days, your loved one will just need someone to listen and remind them that they are not alone. Show them empathy and allow them to recover at their own pace.

A serious car accident can turn a household upside down. Everyone's roles and responsibilities change. If you find yourself in the position of providing daily care and support as the primary caregiver, the following tips may be useful.

Take the time to grieve all that was lost and all that has changed in your life together. Learn to accept the new reality and know that every day will provide opportunities to move forward. Set up a structured plan for your loved one's recovery with the help of their healthcare providers. Monitor and track their progress. Celebrate improvements, however small they may seem.

Your loved one may need help keeping track of appointment times and dates. Help to ensure they get to their healthcare and legal appointments. Once there, ask questions, find out what you can do to aid their recovery, and take notes. If your loved one is attending psychotherapy, attend a session with them to better understand what they're experiencing. Also, through books and online resources, gather knowledge and guidance on their injuries, as well as information on the medicolegal process.

You may need to provide assistance with bathing, getting dressed, and preparing meals. This is a good time to implement healthy diets for the entire household so that everyone benefits. Create new routines with clear support roles that involve everyone in the recovery process. Reach out to extended family and friends for assistance.

It's important that you remember to take good care of your own physical and mental health at this time. You may need to take time off from work in order to care for your loved one. Find out what kind of financial supports might be available. Also, if you find yourself struggling to cope, reach out for emotional support and a good psychotherapist of your own to share your feelings with. Try the stress management techniques I outlined in chapter 6 and practice gratitude and forgiveness.

Help to ensure that your loved one takes any medications as prescribed and that they perform any recommended exercises. Don't allow them to push themselves too much and know that there will be good days and bad days.

If you have children, take the time to gently explain what's happened and reassure them that they are safe and loved. Address their fears and concerns, and encourage them to express their feelings about the new situation. Let their school and teachers know about the accident and any household changes.

As a friend to an injured loved one, be honest about the kind of care and support you can offer. At first, it may be difficult to accept what has happened to them. They may be in denial about the severity or extent of their injuries, they may not feel comfortable sharing their experience, and they may be suffering from injuries that are not visible. Don't be afraid to ask questions in order to understand how you can best be there for them as they recover. Ask what you can do to help.

You may need to explore new ways of spending time together that accommodate your friend's injuries. Don't take it personally if you don't hear from them as often, or they forget about plans or break them at the last minute. Remember to listen and let them know that you care. Encourage them in their recovery efforts and assist where possible. They may seem like their old self on good days, but that doesn't mean that they are fully recovered.

If they have a TBI, refrain from comparing your own experiences to theirs. For example, if they mention that they are having difficulty remembering things, don't tell them that you forget things too, and that it's normal for them to have memory issues as they get older. It's important that you don't minimize their symptoms. It's also best not to compare their injuries or their recovery progress with others with similar injuries. Again, no two brain injuries are the same.

The care and support you give to your loved one is crucial to their recovery and will make all the difference in how they progress.

See the positive in having an opportunity to develop a closer, often more meaningful, deeper relationship with them.

TIPS

- *Remember to take breaks from caregiving and schedule time for fun activities for yourself and your family.*
- *Try to maintain a good sense of humor as it can help to brighten even the most challenging days.*
- *Know that even if they are unable express it, your injured loved one is grateful for your care.*

14

CHILDREN AND TRAUMA

With accident injuries, symptoms can be delayed. This is true for adults and children alike. The difference with children is that they cannot always explain their problems.

—Steven Babcock [1]

If you are currently suffering from PTSD symptoms, please note that you may find some of the following material disturbing.

CASE STUDY: CRAIG

Craig was fifteen and a front-seat passenger in his father's Honda SUV when an elderly man ran a red light at 50 mph and T-boned the Honda on the passenger side. The impact caused the car to spin 180 degrees and come to rest facing oncoming traffic. The side airbag rocketed into Craig's head.

The last thing he remembered was something dark heading toward his window. He awoke in an emergency room not knowing why he was there. Horrible pain hammered his head, neck, and back, yet Craig had no memory of the accident nor many of the events earlier that day. He knew that he had gone to the movies with his father, but he could not recall what movie they had seen or where they had gone for lunch.

Craig's father's physical condition was similar to Craig's, but his memory was more intact. The man who had run the red light died at the scene.

Before the accident, Craig had been a healthy, popular young man with many friends at school and in his community. Academics came easy for him—he was an A+ student with little studying. He hoped to attend law school one day.

Following the accident, Craig's personality changed. He became somewhat "unrecognizable" to his friends. His intense moods turned dark without provocation. He became emotionally flat and highly irritable. Little things set him off, and over time, his friends withdrew from him. The orthopedic injuries to his neck and back took more than a year to show signs of recovery. He received regular physical therapy and massages and was able to gradually increase his levels of exercise and activity. Unfortunately, his brain took much, much longer to heal.

The burden of providing support to both Craig and his father during their long recovery process overwhelmed his mother and sister. The endless schedule of doctor appointments and medical procedures weighed on the family, who were now acting as full-time caregivers and chauffeurs. There were no vacations, no fun times, and nothing but hard work that continued for months.

Finances were tight. Delays in insurance payments for lost wages created anxiety and lean times for the entire family. Their lives had changed forever, and a dark atmosphere of depression, frustration, and anger hung over the house.

It was not until Craig entered psychotherapy that a light glimmered in an otherwise long, dark tunnel of rehabilitation. His first meeting with a psychologist started a month before he returned to school.

Resuming school was challenging. Craig's orthopedic injuries left him unable to play sports for the year. Because of his brain injury, his study time had to be adjusted—he could only work short periods before fatigue and a splitting headache took over, and he could no longer concentrate. His frustration led to anger, and on several occasions, he put his fist through his bedroom wall.

Craig and his family's stress began to ease as they learned more about the symptoms associated with Craig's brain injury. The education and support they received in psychotherapy acted as life preservers tossed into a rough sea of fear and heightened emotions.

Craig's neurologist referred him for a neuroendocrinology evaluation and discovered a hormonal imbalance caused by the trauma to his brain. He received hormone replacement therapy, which improved his physical stamina, mood, concentration, and ability to absorb new information. A psychostimulant was prescribed that improved Craig's concentration, allowing him to focus on his schoolwork for longer periods at a time. To support his neurocognitive rehabilitation program, he received speech, occupational, and cognitive therapies and was prescribed neurofeedback and special therapeutic prism glasses. Noise-canceling headphones also helped him with the sound sensitivity that was contributing to his headaches, irritability, anxiety, and depression.

Progress, however, was slow, and it was more than a year before Craig's mother saw hints of who her son had been before the accident. Problems with anger management, impulsivity, and poor judgment persisted but slowly dissolved as he received support, guidance, new coping strategies, and hormone replacement therapy.

After much prodding by his psychologist, Craig and his father attended several group therapy sessions for car-accident survivors. The group sessions were liberating for Craig. He discovered that his difficulties were shared by many others and felt "normal" for the first time since his accident.

Looking back at his recovery, his mother, father, and sister, who had all become involved in his psychotherapy sessions, said that receiving care for the emotional and psychological aspects of his injuries had been the most integral part of Craig's recovery process.

Two years after the accident, the family took their first vacation. A sense of relief lightened the load they'd been carrying. Later that same year, Craig met a young woman and began planning for his future. He continued to require support and accommodations for his schoolwork, but he was confident he could manage with the compensatory strategies he had learned. As he continued to heal, his self-esteem and acceptance of his postaccident reality grew and he thrived.

THE VULNERABILITY OF CHILDREN

The May 29, 2017, *New York Times* article by Nicholas Bakalar, "Car Accidents Remain a Top Child Killer, and Belts a Reliable Savior," notes that car accidents are the most common cause of death in children under the age of 15.[2] In motor vehicle accidents between 2010 and 2014 in the United States, 2,885 children died. Most children who died were not wearing seat belts. Of these, 43 percent were unrestrained or improperly restrained, and 13 percent were riding in cars driven by somebody under the influence of alcohol.

The United States has made significant advances in using child safety seats. In most child cases of severe injury or fatality, safety seats were not used or were misused. In developing countries that do not use safety seats, 50 percent of the road crash fatalities are children.

Children are at increased risk of injury when they are not properly restrained in child safety chairs in rear compartments of the car. Rushed and preoccupied with the stressors in their lives, parents will sometimes neglect these life-saving precautions.

When children are in auto accidents, they are often neglected by the healthcare system, despite there being a list of PTSD criteria for children six years and younger. Unfortunately, younger children can't often verbalize their pain and concerns. Preverbal children are ignored beyond examination for broken bones and bleeds. Little research has been conducted on auto-accident trauma in children or on the incidents of children acquiring brain injuries from auto accidents.

Children are vulnerable to brain injuries, but unless gross injuries are evident, they are not screened or monitored for potential unfolding difficulties. Because children rarely talk about the effects of trauma directly, the psychological effects may never be addressed. Years later, problems may surface with no clear connection to the crash.

It is common in my practice to have patients reveal that an auto accident occurred in their childhood. Although research has shown that childhood memories are unreliable as they are changed by various factors over time, my patients' parents were able to corroborate the accuracy of their children's memories. Upon examinations, traces of unresolved trauma from these early accidents can sometimes be found thread through the fabric of their lives.

Lenore C. Terr, a child psychiatrist and professor of psychiatry at the University of California, San Francisco, dramatically demonstrated the inadequacy of mental health intervention with children who have experienced trauma. Terr studied children who, in the late 1970s, were abducted on a school bus and buried alive. The children eventually escaped and were treated at a local health center.

Terr's findings were published in her book *Too Scared to Cry: How Trauma Affects Children and Ultimately Us All.*[3] Soon after the trauma, the children were screened by mental health professionals who deemed them fine because they had no significant physical injuries and no obvious psychological distress. Years later, the lingering effects of severe, unresolved trauma appeared in many of the victims. Terr writes about the terror, rage, denial, numbing, unresolved grief, shame, guilt, and misperceptions that had erupted in various forms. Self-harm and high-risk behaviors were displayed by some of them years after the trauma. Terr also brilliantly documents how post-traumatic reenactment through engaging in ritualistic, joyless games that look like play are common for many children who have endured traumatic events.

There needs to be much more research on how trauma from car crashes manifests in the lives of children and how to better meet their mental health needs. Greater knowledge and awareness would help to prevent them from experiencing more significant emotional difficulties later in life.

OVERCOMING CHILDHOOD TRAUMA

Repetition compulsion is a long-standing pattern of behavior caused by the unconscious attempt to master a traumatic event or events so overpowering that the emotions and sensations have been repressed. Repression is one of the mental defense mechanisms identified and studied by Sigmund Freud.

Freud first wrote about his concept in a 1914 article, "Remembering, Repeating, and Working-Through."[4] He elaborated on this theory in his 1920 work, *Beyond the Pleasure Principle*, in which he identified four ways repetition compulsions operate.[5] Freud wrote about how traumas are repeated in dreams, in children's play, by creating similar experiences in life without remembering the event that happened, and in developing specific character traits.

Terr observed the repetition compulsion in her adult patients who experienced early childhood trauma.[6] She also observed fear; panic; vulnerability; sudden, unexplained self-destructive behaviors; and poor judgment. The "legacy of childhood trauma" can negatively influence adult behaviors and puts the adult at significant risk of experiencing something similar to the devastating childhood event. Terr believes that "acting out" is the adult's attempt to resolve the earlier repressed traumas that continue to impact their psyche.[7]

With insight and awareness achieved through psychotherapy, self-destructive or counterproductive actions can be avoided or contained. Effective psychotherapy liberates buried traumas and saves the mind from having to expend energy on maintaining and managing repression or re-creating similar painful situations.

I believe that the patterns of emotions and behaviors that Terr observed in her adult patients could also present in children who suffer from auto-injury trauma. Children who have survived crashes should be clinically monitored during their childhood and adolescent years and observed for trauma-related difficulties. Psychologically minded pediatricians could perform this monitoring. However, establishing psychological relationships with patients during early development is not common in the American healthcare system. An established relationship with a trauma-informed mental health professional would be ideal for children who have been in a car accident.

Psychoneuroendocrinology is another dimension that should be clinically monitored. Resources to undertake this type of monitoring are not routinely available. The reality and current thinking regarding most children is, "If it isn't bleeding, don't be concerned."

The book *Feelings Buried Alive Never Die*, by Karol K. Truman, reflects the importance of processing trauma.[8] It does not ultimately work well in life to push painful emotions aside in order to avoid the psychological work necessary to integrate them.

For adults who are reenacting childhood trauma, Terr recommends interventions that include learning to connect with emotions through work in psychotherapy and meeting with groups of other survivors to help process the lingering effects of the trauma. To learn that one's reactions are normal and experienced by others is freeing on many levels—particularly in resolving feelings of shame and guilt.

If you currently work with or are interested in working with children that have experienced trauma, Eliana Gil's book *Posttraumatic Play in Children: What Clinicians Need to Know* is an exceptional resource.[9] Gil references the National Child Traumatic Stress Network, which cites the critical elements of trauma-informed therapy for children:

1. safety,
2. self-regulation,
3. self-reflective information processing,
4. integration of traumatic experiences,
5. relational health, and
6. enhancement of positive affect.

Gil's book is written for professionals and focuses on what she categorizes as Type II traumas, which are complex situations of abuse by perpetrators. The Type II concepts can be useful in working with Type I traumas, which, according to this differentiation, would apply to vehicular-accident-related trauma. Encouraging a child to draw or participate in "play therapy" offers a way to dramatize what they experienced and can be helpful. Children can be inspired to revisit unresolved trauma as they pass through advancing developmental stages. Through language, they can better integrate traumatic memories and trauma-related emotions.

More needs to be done to prevent auto-accident trauma to children. We need to help them recover not only physically but also psychologically. If behavioral or cognitive changes are observed following a crash, find a respected and competent pediatric neuropsychologist or pediatric neurologist to screen for issues. If issues are indicated, have a complete evaluation performed. Also, have children treated by trauma-informed mental health professionals who can provide emotional first aid and help to normalize their fears and concerns.

TIPS

- *If your child has been injured in a motor vehicle accident, try to maintain routines as much as possible.*
- *If you remember being involved in an auto accident as a child, check with family members for accuracy, and let your healthcare providers, including your psychotherapist, know so they can best help you.*

15

PREVENTION: SAVING LIVES AND PREVENTING INJURIES

Dare to reach out your hand into the darkness, to pull another hand into the light.

—Norman Blann Rice[1]

In life, more than in anything else, it isn't easy to end up alive.

—Roman Payne[2]

PERSPECTIVES OF AN EMERGENCY RESPONDER AND LAW ENFORCEMENT OFFICER

Curious about what we can do to prevent so many tragic accidents, I went beyond the cut-and-dry statistical analyses and emotionless Centers for Disease Control numbers for a realistic and gritty view of a man who faces the carnage daily.

I interviewed John, a 40-ish-year-old firefighter, paramedic, and part-time police officer who has worked for more than 20 years for a mid-sized, suburban fire department in the state of Michigan. He spoke with me about car accidents: the roles of first responders, the tragedy of the loss of life, PTSD, and his thoughts on prevention efforts. The interview addresses several essential facets of auto-accident trauma: How does exposure to grotesque scenes of life and death affect the first responders? What helps them cope? What are the thoughts of an experienced police officer and EMT on prevention? The names and some identifying information have been changed to protect John's and others' anonymity.

John is haunted by a crash that occurred several years ago. Of the hundreds of accidents he's responded to over his long career, the wreck continues to grip his mind and slow his step. Flashbacks momentarily paralyze him, and intense emotions erupt unexpectedly. He believes reminders of that life-changing trauma will shadow him for the rest of his life.

If you are currently suffering from PTSD symptoms, please note that you may find some of the following material disturbing.

Dr. Z: "What happened? When was this accident? What was involved?"

John: "I remember it was a cold December morning just before Christmas. We had gotten a call of an auto accident on the expressway, on an overpass not far from the fire station. When we got there, it turned out to be a terrible head-on collision.

"A drunk driver had flown onto the freeway going the wrong way. His old Ram truck crashed front to front into a Honda Civic going about 70 miles per hour.

"As soon as we showed up, it was clear the drunk driver of the truck was already dead. He had not been wearing a seat belt and had bounced around like a ping-pong ball in the cab.

"It was kind of a screwed-up response for us because we ran both our fire engines and an ambulance. We were not sure of the exact location of the accident. The engine company committed to one direction, the ambulance I drove took the other. The county sheriffs had already blocked off the expressway. Morning rush hour, along with Detroit's workforce, came to a halt.

"Since the freeway was shut down, my partner and I drove the ambulance heading north in the southbound lane. We had to get there as soon as we could. People needed us. The engine crews arrived a few minutes later. As we surveyed the scene, the cops pointed in the direction of the injured man in the Honda.

"My partner went to the Ram truck, and I went to the Honda. Inside the mangled car, I found a severely injured male in his thirties. It wasn't until later that I learned he was a resident physician on the way to work at one of the major hospitals.

"The drunk driver had crashed head-on into his Honda, and the dash had folded in and crushed his legs. He was trapped in the vehicle. As I moved inside the car's compartment, one of the deputies showed up with an emergency C-spine brace. My partner ran back to us and said the other guy was a Priority 4, which is an emergency triage code for 'the victim is dead.' No critically injured treatment or emergency transport was needed for him.

"I radioed our engine company to let them know what we had and where they needed to be positioned. We had to work both sides to get the dash off this guy in the Honda. I recommended they get another engine company to bring their 'Jaws.'

"Once that happened, I crawled into the back with the patient. He was conscious, and we spent a good 40 minutes talking. He was clearly in shock but told me he was a resident. For a short time, we talked about his family. The unfortunate thing was that he understood the level of the injuries he had—before going to medical school he had been a medic in the army, so despite being in shock, he kind of knew what was going on and it wasn't good. His level of respiratory distress increased because he could feel his lungs fill up. At that point, we knew that as soon as we pulled off the dash, he would die."

"Why would pulling off the dash cause him to die?"

"It was a 'crushed syndrome.' Technically, he should have already been dead. When we pulled off the roof of his car, we saw his level of injuries. That's why we started the IVs in his arms—to replace the fluid he was losing. We knew the trauma below his waist would be devastating. The dash acted as a tourniquet. It was clear that the moment we lifted it off, all the fluids would drop to his legs. A horrible dilemma—we knew that 'saving him' would end his life. He discussed this with me. As each minute brought us closer to his

death, we talked about his family and how much he loved them.
'Promise me you'll find my wife and kids and tell them how much I
love them. And that I'll always be watching over them.'

"It's the worst fatal I've ever responded to. And I've been to a
lot." John's voice quivered, and his straight posture collapsed.

"I'm also a local county police officer. It's my second job. We
see a lot of fatalities. I started fire service over 20 years ago, and
I've seen some hellacious 'fatals.' But having to tell his family that
he loved them and would watch over them crushed me and was
probably the worst thing I've ever had to do."

"This emotional wound you harbor sounds deep."

"It still tears me up. It's a bad memory that is always running in
the background."

*"Did you break the news of his death to his family? Or did they
already know?"*

"They already knew. It was one of those things—as soon as we
got him out of the vehicle, his level of consciousness dropped. Med-
Star and our ambulance were right there, so we said, 'Let's go.' We
threw him in the ambulance. A MedStar medic, my partner, and I
jumped in. The MedStar medics were looking at us kind of in shock.
We just told them to drive. We lost him twice, before we got to the
hospital."

"Where did you take him?"

"To the city Level 1 trauma hospital. He had a pulse when we
walked in; they worked on him for another 30 minutes before they
called him. The sheriff or state police, I don't remember, got the
family down there. I had to leave on another accident run and was
back at the same hospital an hour later with a different patient. I
asked if the family of the resident physician was there and was told,
'Yes, in the grieving room.' They had already notified the family he
was dead. That's when I knew that I needed to talk to them. He had
an eight-year-old boy and a nine-year-old daughter. It was one of
the hardest things I've ever done, telling them their husband's and
father's last thoughts were of them, that he loved them. I did lie to
them, though. They asked if it was painless, and I said yeah, he went

quickly. Truth is he lived almost an hour after the accident, and no, it probably wasn't painless—but I wasn't going tell his family that."

"Did you administer pain medications to him?"

"No, we couldn't. He was probably in so much shock he didn't feel what he should have because of the adrenaline. We can't offer trauma patients pain medication because it masks the symptoms, and they might not be able to tell the ER doctor something hurts because they're not feeling any pain. They don't like us providing pain meds to severe trauma patients. If you break your arm, we can give you something for that."

"Was he talking about death? How did he process that?"

"Yes, he knew it was coming. He was planning for it. He told me to talk to his wife and kids. He kept telling me he knew that he was going to die. I was like, 'No, give us some more time, we'll get you out of here.'"

"He said, 'No, I can feel the blood in my lungs.'

"I said, 'Okay, we can fix that.'

"'How you gonna do that?'

"We both knew the probable outcome.

"'We can put a chest tube in.'

"I tried to stay positive because when we first got there, he was shouting, 'Get me out, get me out!' He had no comprehension of what had happened or what was going on.

"Because of the damage to the car, we couldn't just pop the door and get him out. And trying to push the dash to one side wasn't enough—he was around 5 foot, 11 inches, 220 pounds in a small car. Trying to roll the dash to one side wasn't getting us enough room, so we had to get the dash on the other side. What should have been a 10- to 20-minute extraction turned into almost a 40-minute removal. It gave him more time to process. I didn't catch it initially, him preparing himself to die. Now looking back, the fact that he said blood was filling his lungs, he was telling me what was going on with him as it happened, which matched the level of injuries we saw once we rolled the dash off him. His comments matched what we saw. That's why we knew to start a bunch of IVs because once we removed the dash, the blood was going to go and hopefully, we could keep enough fluid in him until we got to the hospital, and they would replace the blood he'd lost."

"I can't imagine staying so calm and acting positively in such a horrendous situation." John started tapping his foot. I could see that telling this story was hard on him. His body said it all.

"I'm one of those people that wants to stay positive with patients even when they are checking out. I've always considered being a medic a morbid game. Death on one side, us on the other. Sometimes, death wins. Sometimes, we win.

"We started large IVs, and we were pushing fluids—just trying to keep him alive, trying to stay positive all the way to the hospital. And when we went back to the hospital later that day, the trauma surgeon came down. He told us there was absolutely nothing he could have done. The patient's aorta had been ripped; the car had kept the blood from pouring out. The surgeon said he could have been on the operating table as soon as we got him out of the car, and he still would have died."

"Was he still conscious when you removed the dash?"

"Yes, he didn't become unconscious until we transported him. His level of consciousness dropped as soon as we got him out of the car.

"He said, 'I don't feel anything.'

"I said, 'Okay, we can fix that; you might have broken your back.'

"Then he was getting sleepy, and we were trying to keep him awake. After he arrested the first time, we never got him back to talking. At that point, we were just trying to keep his heart beating."

"So, you were with him for about 45 minutes? Sounds like you really formed an attachment to him."

"Yes, I did. He shared parts of his life with me, which bonded us. We had things in common. A wife, kids, going to work, healthcare. I was an army brat, so when he told me he had been in the army, it gave us something to talk about other than what was going on. And when he spoke about his family and dying, I steered the conversation back to his army days. I wanted to keep his mind focused somewhere other than his close proximity to death."

"In your mind, you knew it wasn't likely he would survive?"

"Initially, I thought he would survive, but when we pulled the roof off and I saw the extent of the damage, it was one of those when you know . . . crap, this is not going to end well."

"You had to saw the roof off?"

"Yes, we had to cut the front and back pillars (they call it rolling the roof). Basically, we flipped it back. Because of his size and the smaller dimensions of his car, we couldn't get him out the doors. It was going to be easier to put the board under him, slide him up, and then down. We got him out relatively quickly. We had a blanket over our heads in the car. We didn't see anything until they pulled off the roof."

"Do you have nightmares about it? Flashbacks?"

"Yes, still do. No sooner do I go for a while not thinking about it, then something happens, and it comes back."

"And the entire freeway was shut down for hours?"

"For hours, because MSP [Michigan State Police] brought their accident investigation team out there. It was a double fatality; we knew that the drunk driver was dead at the scene."

"What happened to him?"

"To be honest, I have no idea; I never saw him. My partner said there was a case of beer with bottles thrown all over the cab of the truck. The guy wasn't wearing a seat belt and looked as if he had bounced around inside the truck. There was no pulse when they extracted him; MedStar confirmed all that. Later, we discovered that he had just been served with divorce papers, and he was a drinker. He was drowning his sorrows in alcohol and got on the freeway going the wrong way. Everyone avoided him until he crashed."

"How do you feel about drunk drivers?"

"I've always hated drunk drivers. Unfortunately, most of the time, drunk drivers end up killing people yet do not die themselves. This was different."

"How many drunk driving fatality accidents do you estimate you've been called to?"

"Geez, 50 plus."

"Fifty drunk driving fatalities?"

"Over a 25-year career, over 50 . . . easily. Probably more. Working in different counties as a fireman, paramedic, and cop has given me a lot of experience. I helped put myself through college by working as a paramedic and as a paid, on-call county firefighter. I ended up with a degree in public safety administration.

"About 20 years ago, I worked for a different fire department; one other collision troubled me. So tragic." John took a deep breath and quickly released it.

"It was prom season. We had four kids speeding through the back roads, drunk as skunks. The driver hit something that launched the vehicle, hit a tree, split the car in half, and killed all four. All of them were killed instantly or were dead when we arrived on the scene. To see those kids dressed in their prom dresses and suits, ready to spring into their lives—it was heart-wrenching.

"The following summer, a drunk guy drove his sports car down a county road and rocketed his car into a tree. He flew into the roof of a house across the street.

"Another time, more drunk young kids driving on a back road, lost control, and crashed into a boulder. We called dispatch for extra help and were told helicopters would be there, but no additional units were available.

"All were drunk. What a waste of life. I can't imagine how the parents get over something like that.

"Around midnight a few weeks ago, a drunk and high young woman was speeding down a back road, lost control of the car, hit a tree, and it blew her apart. I can go on and on with the drunks that I can remember."

"If there are 50 drunk fatality accidents, there must be 100s of others that are not fatalities but still accidents? It's probably a daily thing?"

"Well, like yesterday. We were out in the rain, and people were bouncing off the median walls. I don't know if they were drinking; I just know the fatalities I have been on when drunks were involved. Again, the drunks are the cause and often live. When they've been drinking and are alive, the cops deal with them."

"Do you end up with anger as a result—I mean anger at drunk drivers? How do you deal with that?"

"Working as a cop, I make sure I sign up for every drunk-driving detail when it's available. I have seen a lot of good people get hurt because of drunk drivers, and it's stupid. With cabs and the systems in place to get these people rides home, there is no excuse. Whether it's a cab, bus, designated driver, walk, or whatever. There's no reason for a drunk to drive."

"What percentage of accidents would you estimate could be avoided or prevented?"

"Ninety percent plus. Most accidents occur because someone did something wrong."

"What percentage are from distracted driving in your experience? And what other issues do you see?"

"I would say 70 percent are distracted drivers, especially now with cell phones and texting. When we do a crash report, we classify if it was drunk driving, distracted driving, or special circumstances (an act of God—deer, elk, moose, or whatever here in Michigan). Those are small percentages and can't be prevented. If you're driving down the road doing everything right and, suddenly, a deer jumps out in front of you, there's nothing you can do about that. But if you reach down and grab that cigarette that fell under your seat and hit someone—well, yeah, that's your fault. Or you're busy changing the radio channel, just for a second. That's all it takes. There are only a few I consider 'true' accidents."

"How do you feel about the distracted-driving issue? Do you think enough is being done about that? What more could be done?"

"It's a fine line. Where do you stop before government interferes with personal rights? But at the same time, your rights end where mine begin. If you're not paying attention, and you're too busy texting your friends—I've been coming home from work and have seen people taking selfies, women doing their makeup, guys arguing on the phone—you're asking for a collision. Or the guy who's late for work, so he's flying down 696. I'm doing 75 to 80 mph, and he blows by me. That's an accident waiting to happen. Or in Michigan's winters, you get snow on the freeways. Yeah, it might be plowed, but you still have ice underneath. Someone is running late to work, and they're just zooming by and talking on a cell phone. Personally? I'd love to see cell phones banned in cars. Period. End of story."

"Do you find yourself going around, day to day, just being kind of angry when you see people's behavior with cell phones? And drinking and driving? Does it leave you with irritation, frustration?"

"To the point, it irks me. And I realize that the only thing I can do is change myself and my family. You know, instill responsibility in my kids.

"As I see the things people do on the road, yeah, I say to myself, 'You asshole, you're going to get someone hurt.' But there's nothing I can do about it when I'm driving outside the county."

"I have a couple of insurance questions about drunk and distracted driving. If someone is intoxicated, and they have an accident, is their insurance voided because they were doing something illegal? Do they in effect have no insurance?"

"No, Michigan is a no-fault state, so it depends on their policy. Some insurance companies put in their paperwork 'if you get caught doing something . . . then you are null and void.' Some don't have it, so it all depends. But in Michigan, if you hit me, I can't sue you, or if I hit you, you can't sue me. Your insurance pays for yours and mine pays for mine. And Michigan is the only state in the country that has a catastrophic fund, which we all pay into. Michigan is the only state that requires insurance companies to provide lifetime coverage if some debilitating injury prevents them from returning to a normal life."

"How do you think the problem of drunk driving could be better addressed?"

"I don't know. I don't know if you heard, but probably about 15 years ago, a local cop was on his way home and was killed when a drunk driver hit him. The guy had 13 prior drunk driving convictions . . . *13!* Thirteen drunk driving convictions, and he was still behind the wheel of a car.

"You've got to make the punishment severe enough that people are afraid to do it. But at the same time, the Supreme Court system says, there's a thing called, 'unfair punishment' for a crime, but to me, drunk driving is a serious crime. When you're killing people because you are drunk, it is the same as murder and should be treated the same.

"We had a family of five, a mom with her four kids, killed by a guy who got fired from his job and bought a fifth of whatever. He entered the expressway the wrong way and killed the entire family. Why isn't he still in jail? Because everyone enjoys alcohol, society does not allow the court system and the legislature to impose punishment severe enough to prevent people from drunk driving."

"What do you think about alcohol-related auto technology? For example, if people were made to blow into a device in order to drive their car?"

"I'm all for someone coming up with prevention stuff like that. I just think it needs to get better. The saliva in your mouth carries your DNA; maybe incorporate that into the system, so it knows that it's you, not your wife, kids, or buddy driving the car. They have to do something.

"Problems also come with legalization of marijuana."

"Are there more accidents with marijuana legalized?"

"Yes. Some can smoke and drive, well, you're still impaired. Just because it's legal for you now to consume it, doesn't mean you can get behind the wheel and drive under its influence. I mean the legislature and technology haven't caught up with what level of THC in your system is legal like we have done with alcohol. So, it's up to law enforcement to articulate in their report the level of impairment based on behavior.

"If pot becomes legal in this state, you will see even more people driving under the influence. People under the influence of marijuana drive slowly and are more cautious, but they still cause accidents. You won't see the fatalities associated with marijuana that you do with alcohol, but you will see an increase in crashes because people will not judge their ability to calculate distances, to make proper turns. It is still impairment.

"It's great that states are legalizing pot, but the federal government needs to do so as well so it can be better regulated. The federal government can come up with standards. If you get 3 micrograms, or whatever it is, in your system, then you're impaired, and you get arrested for operating under the influence of drugs. If you have less than that in your system, then you're fine. The federal government sets the standards for drunk driving; they need to do the same with marijuana."

"Do you think we do enough in terms of driving education? What are your recommendations to change how we train drivers?"

"No, driver's education needs to be more realistic. Step 1: drive with an instructor. Step 2: drive with Mom and Dad, you know . . . go out to some place where they have a huge parking lot and say, 'Here's a set of cones, now you're going to text me and drive with me sitting next to you, and you can't hit any cones. Or try to hold a conversation on the phone with me or someone else while driving and don't hit any cones.'

"Show them how they're not able to do both things simultaneously at 16. I can't do it at 40! They need real examples because teenagers think they are indestructible and invincible and that they can do what they want and nothing's going to happen to them. That's why their insurance rates are so high. They think they can text their friends, take selfies, and nothing's going to happen . . . until it does. Give them realistic training."

"I read that more than 50 percent of new drivers have an accident their first year?"

"I would agree. Maybe they've done their road courses with the driving instructor, and they've driven with Mom and Dad. However, they haven't had a realistic driving experience—especially under the pressure of their friends. 'I really want you to call me,' one says, or they're too busy talking to three or four people in the car rather than paying attention to what they're doing. That's just as bad as talking on the phone. So yes, I would probably say that's an accurate statement."

"How would you advise people to deal with all the other incompetent drivers out there?"

"Pay attention! If you see a driver under the influence, stay far away and call 911. Some seasoned officers get annoyed with 'Well, we have a suspected drunk driver on such-and-such freeway.' But then you have officers that will race to the highway trying to catch that person. On the law enforcement aspect, you're going to have half and half. I'm one of those that will rush to get them, especially if the caller stays on the phone and behind the driver, so we can find them. Sometimes the suspects are just tired and not drunk."

"As a law enforcement professional and a firefighter, are you ever interviewed by policy makers? Is there any interaction between you and policy makers or legislators?"

"There is interaction between my chief and me, and the chief and the chiefs' association and the chiefs' association has their lobbyist in Lansing who push for things on the federal level. There's even conflict with that."

"If this is your opportunity to influence policy makers through what you're saying in this book, what are two or three things you would want to slam dunk to them?"

"I would like to see better and more realistic driver training for the kids. That's the main thing. If you give them an authentic sense of what it is to drive with friends talking with you in the car, or texts, or cell phones, they'll see how, in one second, a devastating accident can occur. That might wake kids up a bit.

"Then when it comes to the drunk driving, we have to do something. We *must* do something because we're killing the mom and the four kids; we're killing the dad on the way to work. We're killing these people left and right. We have got to do something. I just don't know what it is."

"They say on a Friday night, there is an amazingly high percentage of people who are driving while impaired?"

"If it's just a typical Friday night and everyone's at the bar, and they live 20 minutes away, there's no easy way for them to get home, so they drive. And you know some of the highest drinking and driving rates of the year? The day *before* Thanksgiving, St. Patrick's Day, Memorial Day, the 4th of July. The huge holidays, where there's lots of drinking, are safer than the day before. There are fewer driving fatalities on the big holidays compared to most other drinking days because everyone's got rides, they know it's a big drinking day. The bars have cabs lined up outside the bar; people have designated drivers. Why can't we do that every weekend? On the big drinking days and holidays, we have these low drunk driving statistics."

"If there's an accident, is everyone tested for alcohol levels?"

"Only under suspicion. The officer has to see something or think that you're under the influence to test you. Two people get in a fender bender outside here, and I can't give them both a field sobriety test to see if either has been drinking. But if one of them gets out of the car with bloodshot eyes, slurring speech, and can't stand straight, then yes."

"What's helped you cope with all the trauma that you're exposed to? What are your coping mechanisms that other paramedics might benefit from?"

"A very sick sense of humor. I didn't believe it until I first got into it. But the fire department, EMS, and cops have a twisted sense of humor. It's a coping mechanism. You just comment or make a joke you wouldn't make in public. Prime example. My first fatality, a lady committed suicide by running into a semitruck, blew the car and herself apart. I was still relatively new to the fire service.

"The medical examiner showed up, and he's got the gurney and a body bag. He puts whatever he had of the body into the bag, and he's walking around picking up the parts. I looked at him, and he said, 'parts are parts' as he put them in the bag. He found a piece of her skull with brain matter and said, 'Penny for her thoughts' and tosses it in the bag. He found her ear, 'Think she can hear me now?' And dropped it into the bag. Just sick . . . stuff that nowadays, we have to be careful what we say. If somebody has a camera and hears that kind of talk, the public will go bonkers."

"Could you be fired?"

"Yeah, but the public doesn't realize that's how we cope. We make light of a tragic situation by making a joke of it, so we don't have to deal with it. I've been fortunate. I have a great wife who understands law enforcement as she's from a family of cops.

"There have been times when at 3:00 a.m. stuff happens. I've had a kid die. I called my wife—spent an hour on the phone with her just venting, and luckily through my career, I've been able to maintain a relatively normal sense of sanity. That one on the highway still haunts me, but it's the only one."

"Would you say that family plays a significant role in maintaining your mental health?"

"God, yes. There have been days when my kids stayed home because I'd had a rough night, and I just wanted to hang out with them. School can wait. It's just first grade and kindergarten. We go to the inside park; it's an inside play structure. I take my shoes off and play around too. Sometimes we take a week off and go camping, fishing, swimming, boating. It's beautiful. My wife is a girlie girl—her idea of roughing it is a Holiday Inn—but she tolerates the outdoor stuff, or she'll just send the boys.

"Family is essential, although I'm not as close to some of my family members as I'd like to be. It's more their choice than mine. And there are some family members—not immediate family members—that I'm close to, and I have friends I consider brothers or sisters because I'm closer to them than some of my family. Family doesn't have to be blood. Those people help. And some are in public safety, and some are not. Some understand stuff that's going on; some don't, but they are all very supportive. They know this is what I do. It helps."

"If you estimated how many traffic accidents you've responded to in your work, what number would you give it? Total?"

"Thousands. And luckily, most are just minor. Unfortunately, most could have been prevented."

COULD SELF-DRIVING CARS ASSIST WITH PREVENTION?

As Adam Luehrs said, "Relinquishing control and putting your life in the hands of a machine is a big step for people to take."[3] But could a machine help to prevent accidents on the road?

Gary, an automotive evaluator for new cars, is not optimistic about the future of autonomous vehicles.

"We have the technology for autonomous vehicles to operate now," Gary said, referring to the vehicles he road tests. "But I don't see it happening full-scale in America for at least another 100 years."

A major problem with cars functioning effectively is that not every driver wants to obey traffic rules and protocols. Gary believes that rude, law-breaking drivers engage in road behaviors that will cause the technology to fail. For example, some drivers cut in front of others in abrupt, unexpected ways. The car behind the cut-in will automatically brake, which can result in accidents. Only with a complete overhaul of highway infrastructure and the requirement that all vehicles operate autonomously, does he see fully automated cars a possibility on the road en masse.

Gary's interests also include taking on the insurance companies and their unspoken policy regarding accidents and traffic laws. He believes that insurance company lobbyists worked to have helmet laws eliminated because it is more cost effective for motorcycle riders to die in road crashes. Without helmets, death is more likely. Better to pay for a funeral than to pay for 20 years in a nursing home. Insurance companies also use the cost of accidents to justify their high premiums.

What would the impact on the insurance industry be if most accidents were eliminated by effective self-driving cars? The economics are interesting to consider. Would the cost of car insurance have to go down because of lower payouts? How would liability issues shift if crashes were not due to driver error, but to product malfunctioning and manufacturing factors instead? Given the financial power of the insurance industry, one thing is certain, I predict their voice will play an important role in the future of autonomous vehicles.

TIPS

- *Before purchasing a vehicle, research its safety rating.*

- *If you must make a call when you're on the road, place the call before you start driving and use a hands-free device to talk.*
- *If you're going to drink alcohol, plan ahead for alternate transportation.*

16

POST-TRAUMATIC GROWTH: OPPORTUNITIES FOUND THROUGH CRISIS

All suffering prepares the soul for vision.

—Martin Buber[1]

The mark of your ignorance is the depth of your belief in injustice and tragedy. What the caterpillar calls the end of the world, the Master calls a butterfly.

—Richard Bach[2]

A NEW DOOR OPENS

There are survivors of collisions who, because of their injuries, cannot continue their current careers. It can be devastating to you and your family financially and emotionally to feel that the years you've spent training, working in your chosen career, and making future plans have all gone out the window. Or perhaps you are just starting to venture out into the world of education and work and now must completely alter your goals. If you find yourself in either position, again, remember that you are not alone.

As with all experiences of loss in life, it's important that you grieve; reach out for support from your loved ones, your psychotherapist, and everyone on your healthcare team. Get help discovering the options available to assist you with addressing your current financial needs—including possible disability assistance through your employer, your insurer, or government agencies. Learn to ask for and accept help wherever and whenever it presents itself. It can be a humbling, terrifying, and difficult process. However, it can also be a beautiful, life-affirming, inspiring process that presents a huge opportunity for you to learn and grow. You will find that as you work through your tears and any anger, all becomes easier. Your life may take unexpected turns and you may find that your values have changed, just as you have undergone enormous changes. You may decide to retrain and return to school, volunteer, work part time or simply retire.

If you're setting out on an entirely new path, enlist the help and support of the people you identify as your care team as well as a vocational rehabilitation counselor. They can help you to research and explore all of the new possibilities available to you. Take a personal inventory on your interests, passions, and hobbies.

You may find that some people in your life fall away, but you will also have the opportunity to meet many new, inspiring people that will not only nurture and enrich your life but also expand your mind and your heart. Your new path could lead you to an even more purposeful, fulfilling experience of life.

INSPIRING SURVIVORS

Jacques Cousteau's car crash nearly killed him and ended his naval career as a fighter pilot. Cousteau's rehabilitation involved aquatic therapy and swimming in the ocean. It was there that he realized his love of the water and his passion for the sea.

He eventually purchased *Calypso*, a ship for his new work. He reconditioned the former Royal Navy minesweeper into an oceanographic vessel and set the stage for his television series, *The Under-*

sea World of Jacques Cousteau.[3] Cousteau's work had a significant impact on raising global awareness of environmental issues and the importance of preserving one of the earth's greatest resources, the sea. Were it not for the horrible crash that ended the fighter pilot's career, we would likely not have heard of the Frenchman whose life work left a tremendous legacy.

Robert, another survivor, was in a horrible car crash on an icy road when a semitruck lost control and collided with his car. More than 10 years have passed since that unfortunate day that ended his career as an automotive industry plant supervisor and left him with permanent physical injuries that make walking a challenge. Often, he needs a wheelchair. He has required numerous surgeries over the years and, to this day, continues physical therapy.

He agreed to talk to my therapy group about his experiences. Despite his challenges, Robert said, "If I could undo the crash, I wouldn't. Because of the accident, I eventually opened doors that had been locked in the past. My relationships changed for the better. I created a new career in photography that I'm passionate about. I'm active in civic organizations and am a speaker and advocate for people living with disabilities."

A few years ago, I met a former surgeon at a continuing education course. She had been in a terrible auto wreck. The moment the collision occurred, she knew her career as a surgeon was over. She was stoic as she told me how she accepted this reality and stayed positive. After recovering from her injuries, she became a dean of a medical school and loves her new career. She uses her previous years of experience as a successful surgeon to help educate future generations of doctors.

If you have become disabled and cannot continue to work in your current occupation, it represents a major traumatic event and loss in your life. Try your best to be open to new possibilities. As difficult as it may be to accept, losing the old job may be a blessing in disguise. If working is altogether out of the question, there are avocations and other activities you can explore to create a new life worth living in which you can thrive.

Stay positive, be open to learning and change, and continue to find and explore your passions.

TIPS

- *Read the previously recommended book* The Artist's Way. *It's a good source for inspiring creative thinking and using your imagination.*[4]
- *Make a bucket list of all of the things you'd like to experience and accomplish.*
- *Redesign and reclaim your life.*

EPILOGUE

I am only one, but I am one. I cannot do everything, but I can do something. And I will not let what I cannot do interfere with what I can do.

—Edward Everett Hale[1]

GLOBAL CONCERNS

From a public health and safety perspective, cars should have been outlawed 100 years ago. However, since this mode of transportation is now a fixture in our world, our only option is to collectively work to minimize the negative health consequences. Significant advances have been made in accident and injury prevention; however, there is still much further to go. Innovative efforts and initiatives to prevent crash injuries are limited only by the extent of our imaginations.

Vehicular road trauma places a tremendous drain on our resources. Although the growing scourge of traffic injuries is acknowledged as a worldwide pandemic and a public health crisis, public policy responses have been characteristically muted at national and international levels.[2]

Global Road Crash Statistics

According to the Association for Safe International Road Travel (ASIRT), these are the grim auto-crash statistics:

1. Road traffic crashes rank as the ninth leading cause of death and account for 2.2 percent of all deaths worldwide.
2. Given the current trends, road traffic injuries are predicted to become the fifth leading cause of death by 2030.
3. Road crashes cost USD 518 billion globally and 1–2 percent of individual countries' annual GDP.
4. In the United States more than 1,600 children under 15 die each year in car accidents.
5. Road crashes cost the United States $230 billion per year.[3]

ASIRT has the following recommendations for policy makers based on the WHO World Report on Road Traffic Injury and Prevention:

1. Identify a lead agency in government to guide the national road traffic safety effort.
2. Assess problems, policies, institutional settings, and capacity relating to road traffic injury.
3. Prepare a national road safety strategy and plan of action.
4. Allocate financial and human resources to address the problem.
5. Implement specific actions to prevent road traffic crashes, minimize injuries and their consequences, and evaluate the impact of these actions.
6. Support the development of national capacity and international cooperation.[4]

According to the World Health Organization, the following actions will save millions of lives and prevent injuries on the world's roadways:

1. Well-enforced road safety laws on speeding, drinking/doing drugs and driving, and use of seat belts, child restraints, and motorcycle helmets.
2. Improved road design.
3. Improved vehicle standards.
4. Better emergency care.[5]

Drivers can help to prevent accidents by

1. refraining from using their cell phone while driving,
2. driving the speed limit,
3. not driving under the influence of alcohol or drugs,
4. not driving when fatigued,
5. staying focused, and
6. teaching new drivers how to drive safely and responsibly.

Professionals treating vehicular-trauma survivors and their families must provide compassionate care, continue to stay on top of current research and developments for effective treatments, become advocates within the judicial system, and promote preventive measures to make our roads safe.

PREVENTION EFFORTS IN THE UNITED KINGDOM

Brigitte Chaudhry's pioneering voice has raised global awareness of road trauma victims. Her son, 26-year-old Mansoor, was tragically killed when a van driver ignored a red light and crashed into him. In 1992, Chaudhry founded the organization RoadPeace in the United Kingdom. The vision of RoadPeace centers on creating "a world where road danger is not tolerated and where road crash victims receive justice and compassion."[6] Through a helpline for victims, the organization offers emotional and practical support along with advocacy.

RoadPeace established a World Day of Remembrance to honor crash victims and their families and to spotlight the global problem of vehicular trauma. The World Day of Remembrance was adopted by the General Assembly of the European Federation of Road Traffic in 1995, the World Health Organization (WHO) in 2003, and the United Nations in 2005. The UN marks the day every November 15.

Chaudhry's success in creating and raising awareness of the global problem of road trauma victimization brings to mind Margaret Mead's famous quote, "Never doubt that a small group of thoughtful, committed citizens can change the world; indeed, it's the only thing that ever has."[7]

INTERNATIONAL DRIVERS

A friend of mine took a vacation in the United Kingdom and rented a car. Confused with driving on the left side of the road, he got into an accident the first day. I once rented a car in Spain and drove to the south of France. I was fortunate not to have had an accident during my first encounter with a European roundabout. Licensing restrictions on driving outside your home country could be helpful. Perhaps international driver's licenses, recognized in more than 150 countries, would be a good idea.

Lessons from a Chicago Taxi Driver

While I was taking a cab from the airport to a brain injury conference in Chicago, the taxi driver, a 60-year-old Iranian and former electrical engineer, mentioned he had recently returned to work following a severe car accident the previous year. A driver had T-boned his cab after dropping his cell phone and, while retrieving it, lost control of the car.

The taxi driver's injuries required months of physical therapy. His ability to enjoy his daily run, which was his one major health and recreational activity, was stolen. He now attempts to exercise by walking, but his mental and physical health have deteriorated.

Prevention Efforts in Dubai

The same Chicago taxi driver had mentioned that he recently returned from a three-week vacation in Dubai where he had rented a car. While driving around the city, he received a text notification stating that he had motor vehicle citations for various traffic infractions. Traffic cameras had captured numerous driving violations. On his first day there, he was issued $450 in fines that were automatically charged to his credit card.

In the *Gulf News*, an article by Ali Al Shouk reported that Dubai's traffic accidents declined from 3.5 per 100,000 in 2016 to 3.2 in 2017.[8] One of Dubai's building projects included an increase in the number of pedestrian bridges from 119 to 169. The intent was to decrease deaths at road crossings with a target date of 2022. There was also a legislative review related to punishment for serious offenses such as running red lights. Even traffic laws to protect unborn children from negligent driving were under discussion. (Dubai considers a fetus a person with legal rights. A mother can be punished if she causes the death of her fetus.) Officials in Dubai stress the importance of using technology to increase road safety. For example, they encourage drivers to use the Dubai Police app to check traffic conditions.

Israel and Honduras

On a recent trip to Honduras, I talked with an artist originally from Los Angeles who lives on a busy, congested city street. We chatted in his art studio while motor scooters carrying helmetless children whizzed by on the beautiful Caribbean island, oblivious to concerns about potential brain injuries were they to crash. The artist told me he had once visited Israel, which had one of the worst driving statistics in the world, until they created a new system like the one in Dubai. Israel now has one of the best driving records in the world.

While doing some research, I found a *Jerusalem Post* article by David Brinn, who reported a 47 percent decrease in road fatalities from 548 in 2002 to 290 in 2012. In Israel, safety efforts such as a

Mobileye warning system, improved road quality, excellent emergency medical treatment, and, in particular, fewer police on the roads, led to the notable decrease in fatalities. Unfortunately, this encouraging trend did a reverse, rising 28 percent by 2015.[9]

Brinn also wrote about a campaign for safer driving called *Or Yarok* (Green Light), implemented in 1997, which involved the Israel National Road Safety Authority installing cameras at dangerous road areas. The number of pedestrian casualties made up 30 percent of the accidents. Trucks and buses were responsible for 20 percent. Authorities stressed that the problem of road safety must be addressed on sociological and educational levels, combined with more stringent law enforcement efforts, including zero-tolerance for repeat traffic offenders.[10]

Tragedy and Void in Namibia

Recently, a mental health professional who works in a step-down clinic in Windhoek, Namibia, e-mailed me. The clinic specializes in recovery of motor vehicle–accident survivors. He wanted to help patients continue healing after being discharged from the clinic.

It fascinated me that my *Psychology Today* blog had reached a clinician in this African nation. He explained that statistical evidence is sparse in Namibia; however, according to WHO, Namibia records one of the highest incidences of deaths from car accidents in the world.

A total void at the clinic exists in the psychological treatment of trauma, and there is no general protocol for providing psychological aftercare to those injured in car accidents. The Namibian clinician finds this absurd. It's well known that the symptoms of trauma are often delayed and prolonged. The injuries can be long-ranging and incapacitating. Psychological symptoms can develop well after the physical wounds have healed. Another worry of his—relatives or immediate family members rarely receive any form of counseling or therapy despite the fact that injuries to one member impact the entire family.

With data from the Namibian Motor Vehicle Fund, the clinician hopes to raise awareness and to address the void in psychological care. He's kindly invited me to take part in a conference that he's planning for both physical and mental health professionals, with a focus on postaccident care.

LESSONS FROM THE EMERGENCY ROOM

I fear it is not only Namibia that has a void in the aftercare of motor vehicle–trauma survivors. I have worked in hospital emergency departments. A psychiatrist once told me about a man treated five times for five separate gunshot wounds. He received excellent emergency medical care, but the psychosocial reasons for repeated injuries of such a violent nature were never explored. He received no counseling to help him to prevent the next penetrating ballistic injury that could end his life. The same can be said for most accident survivors. They receive little to no counseling about the psychological dimension of their trauma and, as mentioned in this book, are simply "treated and released."

Lately, I see more hospital discharge instructions for auto-accident survivors that mention the possibility of experiencing psychological symptoms related to the accident. However, beyond a sentence or two on a paper handout, nothing further is discussed nor addressed.

My work with auto-accident survivors who have sustained traumatic brain injuries and/or post-traumatic stress has revealed that the hospital discharge experience for these survivors is particularly concerning. Often they are not cognitively or emotionally stable enough to drive for some time after their traumatic incident and are at risk of having another accident if they do.

One patient who suffered a brain injury that went undetected for more than six months postaccident shared their experience: "I should have never gotten back on the road without a thorough examination. I often found myself confused and frightened on the road. I had difficulty concentrating, and I was preoccupied with pain and anxiety when driving."

There are now professionals who gauge when a driver has recovered enough to drive safely. In the Detroit area, there are occupational therapists who specialize in driver rehabilitation services. These OTs can both test and retrain drivers to prepare them to return to the roads. It took many years of treating survivors to discover that such professionals even exist. We need more of them. A professional driving rehabilitation consultation and screening needs to be part of a mandatory, postaccident protocol.

SHOCKING STATISTICS

On average, more than six million car accidents each year in the United States result in more than three million injuries, of which two million are permanent and more than 40,000 result in death. Drivers could avoid most car accidents by behaving more responsibly. Regarding highway fatalities, these are the percentages by cause: 40 percent drunk driving, 30 percent speeding, and 33 percent reckless driving.[11]

Child Pedestrian Accidents

Every year in the United States, close to 50,000 children are injured in pedestrian-car accidents, including 1,300 fatalities.[12] Young children are vulnerable as they dart into the street and are often struck.

Many years ago, I saw a toddler riding a tricycle with his young mother. Momentarily distracted, she didn't see her son veer into the busy street. He was killed instantly. I will always be haunted by that horrific event. In this era of distractibility, without our taking extra care or adopting new preventative technologies, I predict that incidences of children being injured or killed as pedestrians will tragically rise.

New Drivers

Knowing what I know about auto-accident injuries, the thought of my children entering the driving age is daunting. Some have said that the definition of a paranoid person is "someone who has all the information." With regard to driving safety issues, I might qualify. A chilling statistic is that 58 percent of new drivers will be involved in an auto accident within the first year of driving. Car accidents are the leading cause of death among young people ages 15 to 29.[13]

TEENAGE DRIVING ACCIDENTS—CONFESSIONS

During my first year of teenage driving, I was involved in two accidents. The first was when I was showing off to friends while driving my parents' only car. We were in a large, empty parking lot. I put the car in reverse and floored the accelerator. I planned to do an abrupt turn around, but the car slammed to a shocking stop when I crashed into the *one* wooden post sticking up. I hadn't noticed the post, but the crunched bumper was hard to miss. The next morning, I waited for my parents to discover the damage on their own. Not good.

The second accident occurred when I allowed my girlfriend to drive my car, with me as co-pilot. She had a provisional driver's permit, and I had recently obtained my full license. While taking a curve on a city street, she changed lanes and crashed into a vehicle that was in her blind spot.

The car was my first—a white-and-black, 1967 Cougar with a red interior. My uncle, who was skilled at auto bodywork, had beautifully restored it after it had been in a dreadful crash. My aunt, cousin, and mother were stopped at a train crossing when a drunk driver smashed into the back of the car. As a result, my aunt suffered neck and back pain for the rest of her life. She never wanted to drive again and passed on five years after the accident. She turned to alcohol to self-manage her depression and anxiety. Family members had expressed concern about her drinking and observed that she was never the same after the accident. Did she suffer an undetected brain injury from the crash and/or PTSD? Sadly, I think both are likely.

In 1972, little was known about brain injuries, and PTSD would not be considered as a possible diagnosis for another eight years. We still have not advanced much in terms of accurate diagnoses for either condition.

HELP FOR TEEN DRIVERS

I always tell teens, "You may be an excellent driver, but you must assume that the other drivers are not." In Michigan, we have an exceptional program offered by the state police that teaches defensive driving. Teens can sign up for the daylong course taught on the Lansing training track. Unfortunately, there is a long wait list. A truly brilliant, innovative course, it should be mandatory for all new drivers, with funding provided by auto insurance companies, auto manufacturers, and government agencies.

Timothy C. Smith, a driving instructor, covers every aspect of safety that parents and new drivers need to know in his excellent book, *Crashproof Your Kids: Make Your Teen a Safer, Smarter Driver.*[14]

There is also a helpful video on YouTube: "Young Drivers: The High-Risk Year." Anne T. McCartt, senior vice president of the Research Insurance Institute for Highway Safety, gives the grim statistics for new teen drivers. Here are some of McCartt's statistics:

1. Crashes are the number one cause of death among teens.
2. Teens have four times the crash rates as adults.
3. Crash rates are higher at night.
4. The rates are higher still when other teens are in the car.
5. The crash rates are the highest right after teens get their license.
6. Crash rates for 16-year-olds are twice that for 18- and 19-year-olds.
7. Crash rates are low with parents in the car.[15]

Why do teens have such high crash rates? According to McCartt, teens underestimate the risks and overestimate their abilities. The formula for a lethal combination is inexperience plus the tendency to take risks.[16]

We must better prepare teen drivers for the risks of the road, both for their safety and the safety of others. Improved driver's education would seem to be a cost-effective investment for our society. My artist friend in Honduras mentioned that part of his driver's education many years ago in LA involved having to watch the graphic documentary film *Red Asphalt*, which depicted horrific images of auto-accident injuries. I know that having my young son watch graphic YouTube videos on the dangers of frostbite had a significant impact on his behavior regarding the practice of wearing gloves in the freezing cold. Maybe *Red Asphalt* should be included in driver's education courses worldwide.[17]

While writing this epilogue, I remembered something from my teenage years that I would prefer to forget. A friend had just gotten his driver's license at age 16. I was 15 and would ride with him on the country roads around our homes and into the nearest town. As we were returning home one night, two friends of ours attempted to pass us on the highway. A competitive spirit overtook my buddy, who prevented their passage until we entered a sharp curve where he then allowed them to pass. They were speeding, lost control of the car, flipped, and landed upside down in a ditch. As we peered into their mangled vehicle, I was sure they were dead. Fortunately, neither of the boys were injured (as far as they knew), but their car was destroyed. My friend and I were horrified by what had happened and our role in the event. Quite shaken up, we chose not to speak of it again.

The story of that accident highlights the inability of new teenage drivers to assess the dangers of the road. All four of us could have become part of the highway fatality statistics that summer night. That accident also illuminates the impulsive nature of adolescence, the poor judgment, and the overestimation of driving ability that can befall 16-year-old drivers. Does the legal age for driving need to be higher in the United States? Perhaps. A better and more prolonged driver's education should definitely be mandatory.

Alcohol and Driving Accidents

We know that alcohol is a major risk factor for car crashes. According to a report by the National Highway Transportation Administration, 22 percent of drivers aged 15–20 who were involved in fatal motor vehicle crashes had been drinking beforehand.[18] Organizations such as Mothers Against Drunk Driving (MADD) have had a significant impact on improving laws aimed at reducing the incidents of alcohol-related injuries. Continued efforts are needed.

RISKY DRIVING BEHAVIORS

Poor driving habits abound on America's roads. The market research firm GfK surveyed bad driving behavior for the AAA Foundation for Traffic Safety in 2017.[19] High incidents of risky behaviors included texting while driving, running red lights, speeding, typing, or sending e-mails. Of drivers aged 19 to 24 years old, 88 percent admitted to engaging in these behaviors during the previous month.

Texting and Cell Phone Use

Cell phone usage causes one in four car accidents in the United States, and texting while driving increases, by 23 times, the risk of a collision. Every state, except Missouri, bans texting while driving. Missouri allows texting if you are over the age of 21.[20]

A brilliant idea would be to require auto manufacturing and cell phone companies to contribute a percentage of their annual profits to provide support to victims of vehicular trauma and to fund auto-accident prevention programs.

Drowsy Driving

According to recent studies by the Centers for Disease Control, as many as 35 percent of Americans are sleep deprived.[21] The American Sleep Foundation reports that about half of drivers drive while drowsy, and about 20 percent admit to having fallen asleep behind the wheel during the past year. A 2009 Massachusetts Special Commission on Drowsy Driving report estimated as many as 1.2 million crashes, 8,000 fatalities, and 500,000 injuries result from drowsy driving each year with annual economic costs estimated at $242 billion.[22]

WHO PAYS?

Auto insurance companies do not want to pay for medical care and are always looking for ways out of providing coverage and paying out benefits. When this happens, medical care falls to government. We need national vehicular-trauma programs, catastrophic funds, and prevention agencies that are well funded. The returns on prevention programs would be staggering.

Let's all do our part to prevent road traffic injuries and make the world safer for ourselves, our children, and the generations to come. As the great Mahatma Gandhi said, "Be the change that you wish to see in the world."[23]

RESOURCES

Please see the bibliography for publication information on all book recommendations listed in the following pages.

TRAUMATIC BRAIN INJURY (TBI)

Acute Concussion Evaluation (ACE) screening tool for TBI, http://www.cdc.gov/concussion/HeadsUp/physicians_tool_kit.html (provided by the Centers for Disease Control and Prevention as part of "Heads Up: Brain Injury in Your Practice" tool kit)

Adventures in Brain Injury, https://adventuresinbraininjury.com/podcasts (podcast by a TBI survivor)

Amy's TBI Tribe, https://www.facebook.com/groups/792052120888627 (informative online support community)

Brain Injury Association of America, https://www.biausa.org

Brain Injury Association of America. *The Essential Brain Injury Guide Edition 5.0*. (guide for purchase here: https://shop.biausa.org/products/EBIG50/theessential braininjuryguideedition50)

Brain Injury Association of America, Information on Brain Injury Specialist Certification: https://www.biausa.org/professionals/acbis/certified-brain-injury-specialist/cbis-information-eligibility

Brain Injury Association of America, "Preferred Attorneys," https://www.biausa.org/attorneys

Brain Injury Canada, https://www.braininjurycanada.ca

Brainline, https://www.brainline.org (all about brain injury and PTSD)

The Brain Warrior's Way Podcast, https://brainwarriorswaypodcast.com/episodes/brain-injury (podcast episodes on brain injury by a leading American psychiatrist and nurse/health expert)

Concussion, starring Will Smith (inspiring film about CTE, concussions, and the NFL, available on Amazon Prime Video)[1]

Conquering Concussion: Healing TBI Symptoms with Neurofeedback and without Drugs, by Mary Lee Esty and C. M. Shifflett (book recommendation)

Designs for Strong Minds, Donalee Markus, Ph.D., https://www.designsforstrongminds.com (programs for neurorehabilitation)

The Ghost in My Brain: How a Concussion Stole My Life and How the New Science of Brain Plasticity Helped Me Get It Back, by Clark Elliott (book recommendation)

Head Cases: Stories of Brain Injury and Its Aftermath, by Michael P. Mason (book recommendation)

Headway, the Brain Injury Association, https://www.headway.org.uk

The Joe Rogan Experience, https://www.jrepodcast.com/guest/andrew-marr (Joe Rogan podcasts featuring Andrew Marr and Dr. Mark Gordon on TBIs and neuroendocrinology)

Kids, Sports, and Concussions: A Guide for Coaches and Parents, by William P. Meehan III (book recommendation)

Living with Brain Injury: A Guide for Families, by Richard C. Senelick and K. Dougherty (book recommendation)

Millennium Health Centers, Dr. Mark L. Gordan, neuroendocrinologist, http://www.tbihelpnow.org (TBI and trauma treatment)

My Beautiful Broken Brain (inspiring, personal documentary film on Lotje Sodderland's stroke recovery, available on Netflix)[2]

National Brain Injury Information Center, 1 (800) 444-6443

National Institute of Neurological Disorders and Stroke, https://www.ninds.nih.gov (traumatic brain injury information page)

Post Concussion Syndrome (PCS & PPCS) & MTBI Awareness Worldwide, https://www.facebook.com/groups/113072042059485 (online support group)

Quiet Explosions, Jerri Sher (producer/writer/director), https://quietexplosions.com (amazing documentary film about traumatic brain injury recovery based on Andrew and Adam Marr's book *Tales from the Blast Factory*, featuring the work of Dr. Mark Gordon)

Spinal CSF Leak Foundation, https://spinalcsfleak.org (information and resources on cerebrospinal leaks)

Tales from the Blast Factory: A Brain Injured Special Forces Green Beret's Journey Back from the Brink, by Andrew Marr and Adam Marr (book recommendation). (Also visit Warrior Angels Foundation, https://www.WAFTBI.org .)

When Brains Collide, by Michael D. Lewis (book recommendation)

POST-TRAUMATIC STRESS DISORDER

DSM-5 Criteria for PTSD, https://www.brainline.org/article/dsm-5-criteria-ptsd

The Evil Hours: A Biography of Post-Traumatic Stress Disorder, by David J. Morris (book recommendation)

Life after PTSD, https://lnns.co/StQqbZ1UdAw (podcast)

National Center for PTSD, https://www.ptsd.gov

PTSD and Mild Traumatic Brain Injury, ed. J. J. Vasterling, R. Bryant, and T. Keane (book recommendation)

PAIN

American Chronic Pain Association, https://www.theacpa.org
Dynamic Neural Retraining System, https://retrainingthebrain.com (brain retraining for healing and managing chronic pain)
"Interview with Dr. John Sarno on His Book *The Divided Mind*," https://youtu.be/mzOBa-t6Vcw
My Neck Hurts! Nonsurgical Treatments for Neck and Upper Back Pain, by Martin T. Taylor (book recommendation)
The Pain Detective: Every Ache Tells a Story—Understanding How Stress and Emotional Hurt Become Chronic Physical Pain, by H. M. Finestone (book recommendation)

SUICIDE PREVENTION

International Suicide Hotlines, http://www.suicide.org/international-suicide-hotlines.html
National Suicide Prevention Lifeline, 1 (800) 273-8255, https://suicideprevention lifeline.org
Online Lifeline Crisis Chat, https://suicidepreventionlifeline.org/chat/
Suicide Prevention, Awareness, and Support, http://www.suicide.org

TRAUMA HEALING

Accessing the Healing Power of the Vagus Nerve: Self-Help Exercises for Anxiety, Depression, Trauma, and Autism, by S. Rosenberg (book recommendation)
The Artist's Way: A Spiritual Path to High Creativity, by Julia Cameron (book recommendation)
The Biology of Belief: Unleashing the Power of Consciousness, Matter & Miracles, by Bruce H. Lipton (book recommendation)
Crash Course: A Self-Healing Guide to Auto Accident Trauma & Recovery, by D. P. Heller and L. Heller (book recommendation)
The Fellowship of the River: A Medical Doctor's Exploration into Traditional Amazonian Plant Medicine, by Joseph Tafur (book recommendation)
Forgive for Good, by F. Luskin (book recommendation)
"How to Transform Your Life," by Dr. Wayne Dryer, https://youtu.be/XvCmW9GKyd0 (inspiration for post-traumatic personal growth)
In an Instant: A Family's Journey of Love and Healing, by Lee Woodruff and Bob Woodruff (book recommendation)
The Mind Unleashed, http://themindunleashed.com (source for inspiring articles)
Miracle Mindset, by J. J. Virgin (book recommendation)
National Child Traumatic Stress Network, https://www.nctsn.org
The New Normal, Dr. James Zender, https://drjameszender.com/blog (*Psychology Today* blog, on Healthline's list of best traumatic brain injury blogs for 2019)
On Grief and Grieving, by Dr. Elisabeth Kübler-Ross (book recommendation)
Positivity, by B. L. Fredrickson (book recommendation)

Posttraumatic Play in Children: What Clinicians Need to Know, by Eliana Gil (book recommendation)

RoadPeace, http://www.roadpeace.org (charity for road crash victims in the UK), 0845 4500 355 (helpline)

Secrets of the Talking Jaguar: A Mayan Shaman's Journey to the Heart of the Indigenous Soul, by M. Prechtel (book recommendation)

Trauma and Recovery: The Aftermath of Violence—from Domestic Abuse to Political Terror, by J. Herman (book recommendation)

The Trauma Therapist, https://www.thetraumatherapistproject.com/podcasts (podcast)

You Are the Placebo: Making Your Mind Matter, by Dr. Joe Dispenza (book recommendation)

RELAXATION, MEDITATION, AND SLEEP

"Guided Imagery for Stress Reduction with Belleruth Naparstek," https://youtu.be/iyyd4MOI_R8 ; https://www.healthjourneys.com/audio-library (Belleruth's audio library of guided imagery and guided meditations for purchase)

"Healing Meditation Music at 432 Hz," https://youtu.be/4wtG01ymIjE

Jason Stephenson's Sleep Meditation Music, https://www.youtube.com/channel/UCqPYhcdFgrlUXiGmPRAej1w (soothing guided meditation, visualization, relaxation, and hypnosis recordings)

Kelly Howell: The Brain Whisperer, https://www.brainsync.com/about-us/about-kelly-howell.html (guided healing meditation programs)

Linda Hall Meditation, https://www.youtube.com/user/AudioMeditation (guided meditations for relaxation and inspiration)

Master Your Sleep: Proven Methods Simplified, by Tracey I. Marks (book recommendation)

Michael Sealey, https://www.youtube.com/user/MichaelSealey (soothing guided meditation, visualization, relaxation and hypnosis recordings)

"Mindfulness Daily," Jack Kornfield, https://jackkornfield.com/event/mindfulness-daily

"Real Way to Practice Self-Love," Louise Hay, https://youtu.be/m8gHWQCZQD4 , https://www.louisehay.com/tag/self-love

"Sleep Hygiene," National Sleep Foundation, https://www.sleepfoundation.org/articles/sleep-hygiene

Spotify music playlists, "The Most Relaxing Playlist in the World," "Spa Music Relaxation," "anti-anxiety myndstream" (music and soundscapes for mindfulness, healing, meditation and relaxation)

Transcendental Meditation resources, https://www.tm.org

"Whole Body Regeneration—Full Body Healing, Emotional & Physical Healing," https://www.youtube.com/watch?v=hdmvMc7TZn0 (Solfeggio Frequency Healing Recording)

HORMONES AND NEUROENDOCRINOLOGY

British Society for Neuroendocrinology, https://www.neuroendo.org.uk

Endocrine Society, https://www.endocrine.org (6,500 endocrinologists and a referral network)

European Neuroendocrine Association, https://www.eneassoc.org
The Hormone Factor in Mental Health, by L. M. Rio (book recommendation)
Hormone Health Network, https://www.hormone.org
Hormone Therapy, Jill Stocker, https://www.drjillstocker.com
International Society for Psychoneuroendocrinology, www.ispne.net
Pituitary Society, www.pituitarysociety.org
Society for Behavioral Neuroendocrinology, https://sbn.org

VEHICLE SAFETY AND AUTO-ACCIDENT PREVENTION

American Bus Association, https://www.buses.org
American Trucking Associations, https://www.trucking.org
Association for the Advancement of Automotive Medicine, https://www.aaam.org
Association for Safe International Road Travel, http://www.asirt.org
AutoNoFaultLaw.com, http://www.autonofaultlaw.com (an informative website that includes pending legal cases that will impact no-fault law in Michigan)
ChecktoProtect, https://www.checktoprotect.org (Check if there are recalls on your vehicle; if so, fix recalls immediately.)
Coalition Protecting Auto No-Fault (CPAN), www.cpan.us (information on Michigan's no-fault insurance issues)
Crashproof Your Kids: Make Your Teen a Safer, Smarter Driver, by Timothy C. Smith (book recommendation)
Drive It Home, http://www.driveithome.org (resources regarding teen driving habits)
European Federation of Road Traffic Victims (FEVR), https://fevr.org
Families for Safe Streets, http://transalt.org/familiesforsafestreets (provides a collection of supportive resources to help victims of highway trauma), (844) 377-7337, info@familiesforsafestreets.org
"Guidelines for Employers to Reduce Motor Vehicle Crashes," https://www.osha.gov/Publications/motor_vehicle_guide.html
International Road Victims' Partnership (IRVP), https://www.irvp.org
Michigan Trauma Coalition, https://mitrauma.org
MyCarDoesWhat.org, https://mycardoeswhat.org (information on how to use your vehicle's safety systems)
National Highway Traffic Safety Administration (NHTSA), www.nhtsa.dot.gov
National Safety Council's Road to Zero, https://www.nsc.org/road-safety/get-involved/road-to-zero (program describes how safety professionals are addressing motor vehicle fatalities)
Network of Employers for Traffic Safety, www.trafficsafety.org
Transportation Alternatives, https://www.transalt.org
University of Michigan Transportation Research Initiative, http://www.umtri.umich.edu

OTHER HELPFUL RESOURCES

Amputee Coalition, https://www.amputee-coalition.org
Case Management Society of America (CMSA), https://www.cmsa.org

Centers for Disease Control and Prevention (CDC), https://www.cdc.gov

Commission for Case Manager Certification, https://wwwccmcertification.org (*Note that a code of ethics requires case manager's first loyalty is to the patient.*)

Delay, Deny, Defend: Why Insurance Companies Don't Pay Claims and What You Can Do about It, by Jay M. Feinman (book recommendation)

National Limb Loss Resource Center, (888) 267-5669, https://acl.gov/programs/post-injury-support/national-limb-loss-resource-center

Occupational Safety and Health Administration, www.osha.gov/SLTC/motor vehiclesafety/index.html

The Personal Injury Law Podcast, http://www.thepersonalinjurylawpodcast.com/category/podcast (American personal injury attorney podcast on the legal process and personal injury claims)

Stop Everyday Killers, https://stopeverydaykillers.nsc.org (information regarding the U.S. opioid crisis)

U.S. Department of Education's National Institute on Disability, Independent Living, and Rehabilitation Research (NIDILRR), https://acl.gov/about-acl/about-national-institute-disability-independent-living-and-rehabilitation-research

NOTES

PREFACE

1. A few weeks after writing this preface, Notre Dame sustained substantial fire damage estimated to cost hundreds of millions of euros to restore. The flames destroyed timbers carved from entire forests of trees cut centuries ago to support the roof of the massive cathedral.

2. Adam Marr and Andrew Marr, *Tales from the Blast Factory: A Brain Injured Special Forces Green Beret's Journey Back from the Brink* (New York: Morgan James, 2018).

3. Joseph Campbell and Bill Moyers, *The Power of Myth* (New York: Anchor Books, 1991), 245.

4. National Safety Council, "For the First Time, We're More Likely to Die from Accidental Opioid Overdose than Motor Vehicle Crash," National Safety Council: In the Newsroom, January 14, 2019, https://www.nsc.org/in-the-newsroom/for-the-first-time-were-more-likely-to-die-from-accidental-opioid-overdose-than-motor-vehicle-crash.

5. Chris Cillizza, "Has Donald Trump Had Enough of Anthony Fauci?," *CNN Politics: The Point*, March 24, 2020, accessed March 27, 2020, https://www.cnn.com/2020/03/24/politics/anthony-fauci-donald-trump-coronavirus-task-force/index.html.

1. LIFE AFTER YOUR MOTOR
VEHICLE TRAUMA

1. C. G. Jung, *Collected Works of C. G. Jung*, vol. 7 (Princeton, NJ: Princeton University Press, 2014).

2. Adam Marr and Andrew Marr, *Tales from the Blast Factory: A Brain Injured Special Forces Green Beret's Journey Back from the Brink* (New York: Morgan James, 2018), 65.

3. Viktor Frankl, *Man's Search for Meaning* (Boston: Beacon Press, 1959).

2. COMMON CONDITIONS

1. Dr. Timothy Howard, "Should I Still Go See a Doctor after a Minor Car Accident," Dr. Harry W. Brown's Arrowhead Clinic, accessed September 3, 2019, https://www.arrowheadclinic.com/category/blog/should-i-still-go-see-a-doctor-after-a-minor-car-accident#see-a-doctor.

2. Amanda Donohue, "Whiplash: More Than Standard Neck Pain," American Chiropractic Association, accessed February 4, 2016, https://www.acatoday.org/News-Publications/ACA-News-Archive/ArtMID/5721/ArticleID/116/Whiplash-More-than-Standard-Neck-Pain.

3. Mayo Clinic Staff, "Whiplash," Mayo Clinic, February 5, 2020, accessed March 17, 2020, https://www.mayoclinic.org/diseases-conditions/whiplash/symptoms-causes/syc-20378921.

4. K. S. Kenney and L. M. Fanciullo, "Automobile Air Bags: Friend or Foe? A Case of Air Bag–Associated Ocular Trauma and Related Literature Review," *Optometry* 76, no. 7 (2005): 382–86, accessed June 2, 2019, https://www.ncbi.nlm.nih.gov/pubmed/16038865.

5. Frank Pintar, Narayan Yoganandan, and Thomas Gennarelli, "Airbag Effectiveness on Brain Trauma in Frontal Crashes," *Association for the Advancement of Automotive Medicine* 44 (2000): 149–69, accessed August 6, 2019, https://www.researchgate.net/publication/11789971_Airbag_Effectiveness_on_Brain_Trauma_in_Frontal_Crashes.

6. Ibid.

7. Ibrahim Afifi et al., "Seatbelt versus Airbag Injuries in a Single Motor Vehicle Crash," *International Journal of Critical Illness and Injury Science* 5, no. 1 (2015): 46–49.

8. M. B. Kramer, T. G. Shattuck, and D. R. Charnock, "Traumatic Hearing Loss Following Air-Bag Inflation," *New England Journal of Medicine* 337 (1997) 574–75, accessed October 4, 2019, https://www.nejm.org/doi/full/10.1056/NEJM199708213370817.

9. Masafumi Ohki, Jyunichi Ishikawa, and Atsushi Tahara, "Sensorineural Hearing Loss Due to Air Bag Deployment," *Case Reports in Otolaryngology* (2012): 203714, https://www.ncbi.nlm.nih.gov/pmc/articles/PMC3420767/.

10. V. Nandapalan, I. D. Watson, and A. C. Swift, "Beta-2-Transferrin and Cerebrospinal Fluid Rhinorrhea," *Clinical Otolaryngology and Allied Sciences* 2, no. 3 (June 1996): 259–64, accessed September 22, 2019, https://doi.org/10.1111/j.1365-2273.1996.tb01737.x.

11. Migraine Resources Center, "When to Suspect a CSF Leak in Patients with Headache," *Neurology Reviews*, accessed September 2017, https://www.mdedge.com/neurology/migraineresourcecenter/article/132780/headache-migraine/when-suspect-csf-leak.

12. Cort Johnson, "The 2018 Dysautonomia Conference Pt. II: Could You Have a Spinal Fluid Leak? An ME/CFS, POTS, FM Perspective," Health Rising Blog, July 21, 2018, https://www.healthrising.org/blog/2018/07/21/dysautonomia-conference-cerebral-spinal-fluid-leak-pots-me-cfs-fibromyalgia/; S. Ishikawa et al., "Epidural Blood Patch Therapy for Chronic Whiplash-Associated Disorder," *Anesthesia & Analgesia* 105-3 (September 2007): 809–814, https://europepmc.org/article/med/17717243.

13. Spinal CSF Leak Foundation, "Diagnosis," Spinal CSF Leak Foundation, accessed September 22, 2019, https://spinalcsfleak.org/about-spinal-csf-leaks/diagnosis/.

14. National Institute of Mental Health, "Post-Traumatic Stress Disorder," National Institute of Mental Health, May 2019, accessed November 19, 2019, https://www.nimh.nih.gov/health/topics/post-traumatic-stress-disorder-ptsd/index.shtml.

3. WHAT IS POST-TRAUMATIC STRESS?

1. Bessel A. van der Kolk, *The Body Keeps the Score: Brain, Mind, and Body in the Healing of Trauma* (Morrisville, NC: Lulu Press, 2019).

2. U.S. Department of Veterans Affairs, "PTSD Basics," U.S. Department of Veterans Affairs: PTSD: National Center for PTSD, accessed July 15, 2019, https://www.ptsd.va.gov/understand/what/ptsd_basics.asp.

3. Edward B. Blanchard and Edward J. Hickling, *After the Crash: Psychological Assessment and Treatment of Survivors of Motor Vehicle Accidents*, 2nd ed. (Washington, DC: American Psychological Association, 2004).

4. D. J. Morris, *The Evil Hours: A Biography of Post-Traumatic Stress Disorder* (Rancho Cucomonga, CA: Houghton Mifflin Harcourt, 2015).

5. Quoted in Ibid.

6. J. E. Sherin and C. B. Nemeroff, "Post-Traumatic Stress Disorder: The Neurobiological Impact of Psychological Trauma," *Dialogues in Clinical Neuroscience* 13, no. 3 (September 2011): 263–78, last modified 2011, https://www.ncbi.nlm.nih.gov/pmc/articles/PMC3182008/.

7. Andrea Park, "Lady Gaga Describes What Her PTSD Symptoms Feel Like: 'My Whole Body Goes into a Spasm,'" *Self*, September 11, 2018, https://www.self.com/story/lady-gaga-discusses-chronic-pain.

8. Hakomi Institute of California, "Method and Process," Hakomi Institute of California, accessed November 18, 2019, https://www.hakomica.org/about-hakomi/method-process.

4. HOW TO DEAL WITH A TRAUMATIC BRAIN INJURY (TBI)

1. Scott Hamilton, "'The Only Disability in Life Is a Bad Attitude,' Meme," Fabric of Digital Life, 2012.

2. Donalee Markus, foreword to *The Ghost in My Brain*, by C. Elliott (New York: Penguin, 2016), ix.

3. T. A. Gennarelli et al., "Comparison of Mortality, Morbidity, and Severity of 59,713 Head-Injured Patients with 114,447 Patients with Extracranial Injuries," *Trauma and Acute Care Surgery* 37, no. 6 (December 1994): 962–68, https://www.ncbi.nlm.nih.gov/pubmed/7996612.

4. Brain Injury Association of America, *The Essential Brain Injury Guide, Edition 5.0* (Vienna, VA: Brain Injury Association of America, 2016).

5. Ibid., 15.

6. Ibid., 72.

7. Ibid., 23.

8. Ibid., 4–5.

9. Ibid., 12.

10. Christine Barba, "How Does Traumatic Brain Injury Affect Dementia Risk?," Being Patient, September 17, 2018, https://www.beingpatient.com/traumatic-brain-injury-and-dementia-risk/.

11. Brain Injury Association of America, *The Essential Brain Injury Guide*.

12. Ibid., 4.

13. Surviving Traumatic Brain Injury, "Fatigue and the Spoon Theory," Surviving Traumatic Brain Injury, accessed November 2, 2019, https://survivingtraumaticbraininjury.com/2015/03/23/brain-injury-resources-fatigue-and-the-spoon-theory/.

14. Mark Gordon and Andrew Marr, "A Paradigm Shift in the Diagnosis and Treatment of Symptomatic Brain Injury," Millennium Neuro-Regenerative Centers, last modified September 2018, http://www.tbimedlegal.com/sitebuildercontent/sitebuilderfiles/WhitePaper.pdf.

15. E. Shorter and M. Fink, *Endocrine Psychiatry* (New York: Oxford University Press, 2010).

16. Shannon Gearhart, "Phineas Gage: American Railroad Foreman," *Encyclopedia Britannica,* accessed June 27, 2019, https://www.britannica.com/search?query=%E2%80%9CPhineas+Gage.%E2%80%9D+American+Railroad+Foreman.

17. William James, *The Principles of Psychology* (New York: Henry Holt, 1890), 220.

18. Clark Elliott, *The Ghost in My Brain: How a Concussion Stole My Life and How the New Science of Brain Plasticity Helped Me Get It Back* (New York: Penguin, 2016).

19. Ibid.

20. James F. Zender, "Omega-3s in the Treatment of Posttraumatic Brain Injury," *Psychology Today: The New Normal* (blog), December 27, 2018, accessed April 1, 2020, https://www.psychologytoday.com/us/blog/

the-new-normal/201812/omega-3s-in-the-treatment-posttraumatic-brain-injury.

21. Ines Vanderbeken and Eric Kerckhofs, "A Systematic Review of the Effect of Physical Exercise on Cognition in Stroke and Traumatic Brain Injury Patients," *NeuroRehabilitation* 40 (2017): 33–48, https://pdfs.semanticscholar.org/d636/0a421f93dc075e97e5052dc13c1094bccbd9.pdf.

22. A. Hadanny et al., "Effect of Hyperbaric Oxygen Therapy on Chronic Neurocognitive Deficits of Post-Traumatic Brain Injury Patients: Retrospective Analysis, " *BMJ Open*, last modified 2018, https://bmjopen.bmj.com/content/8/9/e023387.

23. David Kohn, "Could Hyperbaric Treatment Heal the Brain?," *Washington Post*, January 27, 2018, https://www.washingtonpost.com/national/health-science/could-hyperbaric-treatment-heal-the-brain/2018/01/26/90b3acfa-df87-11e7-8679-a9728984779c_story.html.

24. Wim Hof Method, "Advantages of the Wim Hof Breathing Exercises," Wim Hof Method, accessed November 5, 2019, https://www.wimhofmethod.com/breathing-exercises.

25. Concussion Alliance, "Craniosacral Therapy for Concussion Symptoms," Concussion Alliance, accessed November 10, 2019, https://www.concussionalliance.org/craniosacral-therapy.

26. Brainworks, "What Is Neurofeedback?," Brainworks Neurotherapy, accessed March 18, 2020, https://brainworksneurotherapy.com/what-is-neurofeedback.

27. Reza Ehsanian, "New Treatments in Traumatic Brain Injury: A Clinical Trial of Repetitive Transcranial Magnetic Stimulation," Association of Academic Physiatrists, March 1, 2018, https://medium.com/physiatry/new-treatments-in-traumatic-brain-injury-a-clinical-trial-of-repetitive-transcranial-magnetic-929282c6b5b2.

28. Julie Bowen, "Stem Cell Therapy for Traumatic Brain Injury?," *Neurology Times*, last modified April 19, 2019, https://www.neurologytimes.com/tbi/stem-cell-therapy-traumatic-brain-injury.

29. E = mc Jamo, "Humpty Dumpty and the Second Law of Thermodynamics," *EMCJamo blogspot*, accessed May 30, 2019, http://emcjamo.blogspot.com/search?q=humpty+dumpty.

30. Ernest Hemingway, *A Farewell to Arms* (New York: Scribner, 1995), 267.

31. Ernest Hemingway, *By-Line: Ernest Hemingway: Selected Articles and Dispatches of Four Decades*, ed. William White (New York, Scribner, 1998), 199.

5. A RIVER OF PAIN

1. Albert Schweitzer, *On the Edge of the Primeval Forest*, 2.02 ed. (Acton, MA: Actonian Press, 2010).

2. Ian McEwan, *Atonement: A Novel* (New York: Anchor Books, 2007).

3. J. J. Bonica, "History of Pain Concepts and Pain Therapy," *Mount Sinai Journal of Medicine* 58, no. 3 (1991): 191–202, https://www.ncbi.nlm.nih.gov/pubmed/1875956.

4. Michael E. Howard, *Managing Chronic Pain, Part 1: Types of Pain & Pain Pathways* (Concord, CA: Institute for Natural Resources, 2015), 9.

5. H. Merskey and N. Bogduk, *Classification of Chronic Pain: Description of Chronic Pain Syndromes and Definition of Pain Terms* (Seattle, WA: IASP Press, 1994).

6. John Sarno, *Mind over Back Pain* (New York: Berkley Books, 1999).

7. Alan S. Cowen and Dacher Keltner, "Self-Report Captures 27 Distinct Categories of Emotion Bridged by Continuous Gradients," *PNAS* 114, no. 38 (September 5, 2017): E7900–E7909, accessed April 2, 2020, https://doi.org/10.1073/pnas.1702247114.

8. January Nelson, "A List of Emotions and Facial Expressions," Thought Catalog, last updated July 29, 2018, accessed April 2, 2020, https://thoughtcatalog.com/january-nelson/2018/06/list-of-emotions/.

9. R. Melzack and P. D. Wall, "Pain Mechanisms: A New Theory," *Science* 150, no. 3699 (November 19, 1965): 971–79, https://www.ncbi.nlm.nih.gov/pubmed/5320816.

10. H. Selye, *Stress* (Montreal: Acta Medical, 1950).

11. Ibid.

12. Judy Foreman, *A Nation in Pain: Healing Our Biggest Health Problem* (New York: Oxford University Press, 2014).

13. Pat Anson, "CDC: 50 Million Americans Have Chronic Pain," *Pain News Network*, September 13, 2018, https://www.painnewsnetwork.org/stories/2018/9/13/cdc-50-million-americans-have-chronic-pain.

14. Megan Brooks, "Chronic Pain Now Affects 50 Million US Adults," *Medscape Medical News,* September 8, 2018, accessed October 3, 2019, https://www.medscape.com/viewarticle/902197.

15. Anson, "CDC: 50 Million Americans Have Chronic Pain."

16. Yong Tai Wang et al., "Tai-Chi, Yoga, and Qigong as Mind-Body Exercises," *Evidence-Based Complementary and Alternate Medicine,* last modified January 5, 2017, https://www.hindawi.com/journals/ecam/2017/8763915/.

17. Penny Furness et al., "What Causes Fibromyalgia: An Online Survey of Patient Perspectives," *Health Psychology Open* 5, no. 2 (July–December 2018): 2055102918802683, accessed September 27, 2018, https://www.ncbi.nlm.nih.gov/pmc/articles/PMC6158621/.

6. MANAGING YOUR PAIN

1. Martin T. Taylor, *My Neck Hurts! Nonsurgical Treatments for Neck and Upper Back Pain* (Baltimore: Johns Hopkins University Press, 2010).

2. Ibid., 114–16.

3. S. Mohammed and J. S. Yu. "Platelet-Rich Plasma Injections: An Emerging Therapy for Chronic Discogenic Low Back Pain," *Journal of Spine Surgery* 4 , no. 1 (March 2018): 115–22, accessed March 4, 2018, https://www.ncbi.nlm.nih.gov/pmc/articles/PMC5911760/.

4. Taylor, *My Neck Hurts!,* 114–16.

5. J. Takasaki et al., "Examination of the Effect of Anesthesia on Radiofrequency Ablation of Hepatocellular Carcinoma—a Patient Survey on Radiofrequency Ablation," *Gan To KagakuRyoho* 39, no. 12 (November 2012): 1843–45, https://www.ncbi.nlm.nih.gov/pubmed/23267905.

6. Taylor, *My Neck Hurts!,* 114–16.

7. Korin Miller, "What Is Naloxone?," *Women's Health Magazine,* March 22, 2018, https://www.womenshealthmag.com/health/a19562876/what-is-naloxone/.

8. Debra Houry, "New Data Show Growing Complexity of Drug Overdose Deaths in America," CDC, accessed December 21, 2018, https://www.cdc.gov/media/releases/2018/p1221-complexity-drug-overdose.html.

9. National Safety Council, "Your Odds of Dying from an Accidental Opioid Overdose Continue to Be Greater than Dying in a Motor-Vehicle

Crash," Injury Facts, accessed March 18, 2020, https://injuryfacts.nsc.org/all-injuries/preventable-death-overview/odds-of-dying/.

10. Houry, "New Data Show Growing Complexity of Drug Overdose Deaths in America."

11. David Hanscom, *Back in Control: A Surgeon's Roadmap Out of Chronic Pain* (Seattle, WA: Vertus Press, 2017).

12. John Sarno, *Mind over Back Pain* (New York: Berkley Books, 1999).

13. "Interview with Dr. John Sarno on His Book *The Divided Mind*," YouTube video, 26:26, posted by Paul Mabry, April 29, 2017, accessed November 16, 2019, https://youtu.be/mzOBa-t6Vcw.

14. Howard Schubiner and Michael Betzold, *Unlearn Your Pain*, 3rd ed. (Pleasant Ridge, MI: Mind Body Publishing, 2013).

15. Chron99, "Healing Waters of Mt. Clemens, Michigan," StreetDirectory.com, accessed November 10, 2019, https://www.streetdirectory.com/travel_guide/153764/science/healing_waters_of_mt_clemens_michigan.html.

16. Julia Cameron, *The Artist's Way: A Spiritual Path to Higher Creativity* (Los Angeles: TarcherPerigee, 1992).

17. Wayne W. Dyer, "Finding Meaning in Challenging Times," in *Dr. Wayne W. Dyer Podcast*, podcast audio, May 26, 2019, https://www.iheart.com/podcast/286-dr-wayne-w-dyer-pod-28854940/episode/dr-wayne-w-dyer-finding-43175142.

18. Mayo Clinic, "Hypnosis," Mayo Clinic, accessed October 3, 2019, https://www.mayoclinic.org/tests-procedures/hypnosis/about/pac-20394405.

19. J. Dispenza, *You Are the Placebo: Making Your Mind Matter* (Carlsbad, CA: Hay House, 2014).

20. Herbert Benson and Miriam Z. Klipper, *The Relaxation Response* (New York: Avon, 1975).

21. Bruce H. Lipton, *The Biology of Belief: Unleashing the Power of Consciousness, Matter & Miracles* (Carlsbad, CA: Hay House, 2008), 229.

7. POSITIVE PSYCHOLOGY

1. Viktor Frankl, *Man's Search for Meaning* (Boston: Beacon Press, 1959), 86.

2. Catarina Lino, "Positive Psychology: An Introduction," Positive Psychology, accessed November 11, 2019, https://positivepsychology.com/positive-psychology-an-introduction-summary/.

3. William Ely Hil, *My Wife and My Mother-in-Law*, cartoon drawing, Puck, 1915.

4. Unknown, *Rabbit-Duck Illusion*, cartoon drawing, *Fliegende Blätter*, 1892.

5. D. J. Morris, *The Evil Hours: A Biography of Post-Traumatic Stress Disorder* (Rancho Cucomonga, CA: Houghton Mifflin Harcourt, 2015), 15.

6. Catarina Lino, "Broaden-and-Build Theory of Positive Emotions," PositivePsychology.com, March 7, 2019, https://positivepsychology.com/broaden-build-theory/.

7. Karl Paul Reinhold Niebuhr, "The Serenity Prayer," *AA Grapevine*, January 1950, 6–7.

8. M. K. Gandhi quoted in K. K. Ganguly, "Life of M. K. Gandhi: A Message to Youth of Modern India," *Indian Journal of Medical Research* 149, Suppl 1 (January 2019): S145–51, https://www.ncbi.nlm.nih.gov/pmc/articles/PMC6515741/.

9. Jennifer Sweeton, "Here's Your Brain on Trauma," *Jennifer Sweeton Blog*, February 23, 2017, https://www.jennifersweeton.com/blog/2017/3/14/heres-your-brain-on-trauma.

10. Louis Cozolino, *The Neuroscience of Psychotherapy: Healing the Social Brain*, 2nd ed. (New York: W. W. Norton, 2010).

8. THE POWER OF EMPATHY

1. Robert Weisz, "Attention Is Love," Mindfulness Based Emotional Processing, accessed November 2, 2019, https://mindfulnessbasedemotionalprocessing.com/new-client-forms/.

2. Ernest Hemingway, *A Farewell to Arms* (New York: Scribner, 1995), 267.

3. Dr. Robert Weisz, "Episode 03 P2W: Brainspotting," YouTube video, 27:07, posted by Dr. Christian O'Neill, March 16, 2013, accessed September 5, 2019, https://youtu.be/53NeelMCW24.

4. Gabor Maté, *In the Realm of the Hungry Ghosts: Close Encounters with Addiction* (Berkeley, CA: North Atlantic Books, 2010).

5. John Newton and William Cowper, "Amazing Grace," in *Olney Hymns* (Church of England, 1779).

6. Eva Cassidy, "Fields of Gold," track 8 on *Live at Blues Alley*, Eva Music, 1996, compact disc.

7. Martin Prechtel, *Secrets of the Talking Jaguar: Memoirs from the Living Heart of a Mayan Village* (New York: TarcherPerigee, 1999).

8. J. D. Lindy, "The Trauma Membrane and Other Clinical Concepts Derived from Psychotherapeutic Work with Survivors of Natural Disasters," *Psychiatric Annals* 15, no. 3 (1985): 153–60, https://doi.org/10.3928/0048-5713-19850301-06.

9. Louise Hay, "Real Way to Practice Self-Love," YouTube video, 9:59, posted by Guided Meditation and More with Aditii, March 27, 2018, https://youtu.be/m8gHWQCZQD4.

9. THE BENEFITS OF PSYCHOTHERAPY

1. Judith Lewis Herman, *Trauma and Recovery: The Aftermath of Violence—from Domestic Abuse to Political Terror* (New York: Basic Books, 1997), 1.

2. Brene Brown, "Can We Gain Strength from Shame?," *Ted Radio Hour with Guy Raz*, March 11, 2013, accessed March 19, 2020, https://www.npr.org/transcripts/174033560?storyId=174033560.

3. Jill Stocker, in personal conversation with the author, November 7, 2019.

4. Herbert Benson and Miriam Z. Klipper, *The Relaxation Response*, reissue ed. (New York: Avon, 1975).

10. GROUP PSYCHOTHERAPY—YOU ARE NOT ALONE

1. S. Kelley Harrell, *Gift of the Dreamtime—Reader's Companion* (Fuquay-Varina, NC: Soul Intent Arts, 2014).

11. KEY PROFESSIONALS WHO CAN HELP

1. Commission for Case Managers Certification, "About Case Management," Commission for Case Managers Certification, accessed October 15, 2019, https://ccmcertification.org/about-ccmc/about-case-management.

12. HOW TO DEAL WITH YOUR INSURANCE COMPANY

1. Bill Kizorek, "Investigation of Psychological Claims," in *The Insurer's Handbook of Psychological Injury Claims*, ed. David R. Price and P. R. Lees-Haley (Seattle, WA: Claims Books, 1995), 355.
2. Joseph Tafur, *The Fellowship of the River: A Medical Doctor's Exploration into Traditional Amazonian Plant Medicine* (Phoenix, AZ: Espiritu Books, 2017), 21.
3. Jay M. Feinman, *Delay, Deny, Defend: Why Insurance Companies Don't Pay Claims and What You Can Do about It* (New York: Portfolio Hardcover, 2010).
4. *The Oxford New Desk Dictionary and Thesaurus*, 3rd ed. (2014), s.v. "surveillance."
5. Bill Kizorek, *Disability or Deception* (Naperville, Ill: PSI Publishing, 1986).
6. Sinas Dramis Law Firm, "Michigan's No-Fault Allowable Expense Benefits," Sinas Dramis, accessed March 18, 2020, https://sinasdramis.com/michigan-auto-accident-attorneys/no-fault-allowable-expense-benefits.

13. CARING FOR YOUR INJURED LOVED ONE

1. Joseph Campbell, with Bill Moyers, *The Power of Myth* (New York: Doubleday, 1988), 148.

14. CHILDREN AND TRAUMA

1. Steven Babcock (personal injury attorney), in conversation with the author, August 2018.

2. Nicholas Bakalar, "Car Accidents Remain a Top Child Killer, and Belts a Reliable Savior," *New York Times*, May 29, 2017, https://www.nytimes.com/2017/05/29/health/car-accidents-child-deaths-seat-belts.html.

3. Lenore Terr, *Too Scared to Cry: How Trauma Affects Children and Ultimately Us All*, repr. ed. (New York: Basic Books, 1992).

4. Sigmund Freud, "Remembering, Repeating, and Working-Through," *The Standard Edition of the Complete Psychological Works of Sigmund Freud—Volume XII* (London: Hogarth Press and the Institute of Psycho-Analysis, 1964), 17.

5. Sigmund Freud, *Beyond the Pleasure Principle* (New York: W. W. Norton, 1990), 279.

6. UNM Department of Psychiatry Grand Rounds, "UNM Department of Psychiatry Grand Rounds: Lenore Terr, M.D.," YouTube video, 1:25:52, May 22, 2013, https://youtu.be/czA5X7eTeos.

7. Ibid.

8. Karol K. Truman, *Feelings Buried Alive Never Die*, rev. ed. (Saint George, UT: Olympus Distributing, 1995).

9. Eliana Gil, *Posttraumatic Play in Children: What Clinicians Need to Know* (New York: Guilford, 2017).

15. PREVENTION: SAVING LIVES AND PREVENTING INJURIES

1. Norman B. Rice, *Pass It On*, accessed September 3, 2018, https://www.passiton.com/inspirational-quotes/4813-dare-to-reach-out-your-hand-into-the-darkness.

2. Roman Payne, *Wanderess Quotes and Other Poems* (Boca Raton, FL: Aesthete Press, 2017).

3. Adam Luehrs, "Seven Problems Self-Driving Cars Need to Overcome," Smith's Lawyers, accessed August 13, 2018, https://www.smithslawyers.com.au/post/self-driving-car-problems.

16. POST-TRAUMATIC GROWTH: OPPORTUNITIES FOUND THROUGH CRISIS

1. Samuel A. Nigro, *The Soul of the Earth*, rev. ed. (St. Louis, MO: Central Bureau, 2012), 219.

2. Richard Bach, *Illusions: The Adventures of a Reluctant Messiah* (London: Arrow Books, 1998), 67, http://brainteaser.narod.ru/books/fict/ RichardBach-Illusions.pdf.

3. Jacques Cousteau, *The Undersea World of Jacques Cousteau*, directed by Alan Landsburg, aired 1968–1975, United States, 60 min.

4. Julia Cameron, *The Artist's Way: A Spiritual Path to High Creativity* (Los Angeles: TarcherPerigee, 1992).

EPILOGUE

1. Jeanie Greenough, *A Year of Beautiful Thoughts* (Alcester, UK: Read, 2007), 172.

2. Vinand M. Nantulya and Michael R. Reich (Harvard Center for Population and Development Studies), "The Neglected Epidemic: Road Traffic Injuries in Developing Countries," *BMJ* 324, no. 7346 (May 11, 2002): 1139–41, https://www.ncbi.nlm.nih.gov/pubmed/12003888.

3. Association for Safe International Road Travel (ASIRT), "Annual Global Road Crash Statistics," Association for Safe International Road Travel, accessed September 5, 2019, https://www.asirt.org/safe-travel/ road-safety-facts/.

4. Ibid.

5. World Health Organization (WHO), "10 Facts about Road Safety," *World Health Organization : Newsroom*, accessed August 2, 2019, https:// www.who.int/news-room/facts-in-pictures/detail/road-safety.

6. RoadPeace, "About RoadPeace," RoadPeace, accessed November 21, 2019, http://www.roadpeace.org/about-roadpeace/.

7. Sharon Deutsch-Nadir, "Capitalizing on Women's Traditional Roles in Israeli Peace Activism" (Master's thesis, Fletcher School—Tufts University, 2005), 2, http://www.isha2isha.com/wp-content/uploads/2014/ 02/Deutsch-Nadir_Women_roles.pdf.

8. Ali Al Shouk, "Officials Discuss Road Safety in Dubai," *Gulf News,* last modified February 29, 2018, https://gulfnews.com/uae/government/officials-discuss-road-safety-in-dubai-1.2180698.

9. David Brinn, "The Dangers of Israel's Roads: Who Is to Blame?" *Jerusalem Post*, May 13, 2017, https://www.jpost.com/Magazine/Crash-test-dummies-486885.

10. Ibid.

11. Lawcore, "Car Accident Statistics," Lawcore.com, accessed November 19, 2019, http://www.lawcore.com/car-accident/statistics.html.

12. Marvin Malek, B. Guyer, and I. Lescohier, "The Epidemiology and Prevention of Child Pedestrian Injury," *Accident Analysis & Prevention* 22, no. 4 (August 1990): 301–13, https://www.sciencedirect.com/science/article/abs/pii/000145759090046N.

13. World Health Organization (WHO), "Road Traffic Injuries," *World Health Organization: Newsroom*, last modified February 7, 2020, https://www.who.int/en/news-room/fact-sheets/detail/road-traffic-injuries.

14. Timothy C. Smith, *Crashproof Your Kids: Make Your Teen a Safer, Smarter Driver* (New York: Fireside, 2006).

15. Anne T. McCartt, "100 Deadliest Road Days," *Her Highway* (blog), May 18, 2012, http://www.herhighway.com/blog/100-deadliest-road-days.

16. Ibid.

17. *Red Asphalt*, produced by the California Highway Patrol, 1964–2006. Film series.

18. National Highway Transportation Administration, "Drug and Alcohol Crash Risk Study," National Highway Transportation Administration, last modified August 13, 2018, https://www.nhtsa.gov/behavioral-research/drug-and-alcohol-crash-risk-study.

19. Insurance Institute for Highway Safety, "Cellular Phone Use and Texting While Driving Laws," National Conference of State Legislatures, May 29, 2019, https://www.ncsl.org/research/transportation/cellular-phone-use-and-texting-while-driving-laws.aspx.

20. Bart Jansen, "Millennial Drivers Are Highway Hazards, Survey Shows," *USA Today*, February 15, 2017, https://www.usatoday.com/story/news/2017/02/15/millennial-drivers-highway-hazards-survey-shows/97888336/.

21. Centers for Disease Control and Prevention (CDC), "1 in 3 Adults Don't Get Enough Sleep," Centers for Disease Control and Prevention, last

modified February 16, 2018, https://www.cdc.gov/media/releases/2016/
p0215-enough-sleep.html.

22. National Safety Council, "Drowsy Driving Is Impaired Driving,"
National Safety Council, accessed October 12, 2019, https://www.nsc.org/
Portals/0/Documents/Fatigue%20Documents/Fact-Sheets/Drowsy-
Driving-Problem-and-Statistics.pdf.

23. Deutsch-Nadir, "Capitalizing on Women's Traditional Roles in Israeli Peace Activism," 2.

RESOURCES

1. *Concussion*, directed by Peter Landesman (2015; Los Angeles: Columbia Pictures, Lstar Capital, Village Roadshow Pictures, Scott Free Pro-
ductions/Sony Pictures, 2016), DVD/Blu-ray.

2. *My Beautiful Broken Brain*, directed by Sophie Robinson and Lotje
Sodderland (2014; United Kingdom: Sophie Robinson/IDIFA, Netflix,
2016), streaming on Netflix March 18, 2016.

BIBLIOGRAPHY

Afifi, Ibrahim, El-Menyar, Ayman, Al-Thani, Hassan, and Peralta, Ruben. "Seatbelt versus Airbag Injuries in a Single Motor Vehicle Crash." *International Journal of Critical Illness and Injury Science* 5, no. 1 (2015): 46–49.

Al Shouk, Ali. "Officials Discuss Road Safety in Dubai." *Gulf News.* Last modified February 29, 2018. https://gulfnews.com/uae/government/officials-discuss-road-safety-in-dubai-1.2180698.

Anson, Pat. "CDC: 50 Million Americans Have Chronic Pain." *Pain News Network.* September 13, 2018. https://www.painnewsnetwork.org/stories/2018/9/13/cdc-50-million-americans-have-chronic-pain.

Association for Safe International Road Travel (ASIRT). "Annual Global Road Crash Statistics." Association for Safe International Road Travel. Accessed September 5, 2019. https://www.asirt.org/safe-travel/road-safety-facts.

Bach, Richard. *Illusions: The Adventures of a Reluctant Messiah.* London: Arrow Books, 1998. http://brainteaser.narod.ru/books/fict/RichardBach-Illusions.pdf.

Bakalar, Nicholas. "Car Accidents Remain a Top Child Killer, and Belts a Reliable Savior." *New York Times.* May 29, 2017. https://www.nytimes.com/2017/05/29/health/car-accidents-child-deaths-seat-belts.html.

Barba, Christine. "How Does Traumatic Brain Injury Affect Dementia Risk?" Being Patient. September 17, 2018. https://www.beingpatient.com/traumatic-brain-injury-and-dementia-risk.

Benson, Herbert, and Klipper, Miriam Z. *The Relaxation Response.* New York: Avon, 1975.

Blanchard, E. B., and Hickling, E. J. *After the Crash: Psychological Assessment and Treatment of Survivors of Motor Vehicle Accidents.* 2nd ed. Washington, DC: American Psychological Association, 2004.

Bonica, J. J. "History of Pain Concepts and Pain Therapy." *Mount Sinai Journal of Medicine* 58, no. 3 (1991): 191–202. https://www.ncbi.nlm.nih.gov/pubmed/1875956.

Bowen, Julie. "Stem Cell Therapy for Traumatic Brain Injury?" *Neurology Times.* Last modified April 19, 2019. https://www.neurologytimes.com/tbi/stem-cell-therapy-traumatic-brain-injury.

Brain Injury Association of America. *The Essential Brain Injury Guide, Edition 5.0.* Vienna, VA: Brain Injury Association of America, 2016.

Brainworks. "What Is Neurofeedback?" Brainworks Neurotherapy. Accessed March 18, 2020. https://brainworksneurotherapy.com/what-is-neurofeedback.

Brinn, David. "The Dangers of Israel's Roads: Who Is to Blame?" *Jerusalem Post.* May 13, 2017. https://www.jpost.com/Magazine/Crash-test-dummies-486885.

Brooks, Megan. "Chronic Pain Now Affects 50 Million US Adults." *Medscape Medical News.* September 8, 2018. Accessed October 3, 2019. https://www.medscape.com/viewarticle/902197.

Brown, Brene. "Can We Gain Strength from Shame?" *Ted Radio Hour with Guy Raz.* March 11, 2013. Accessed March 19, 2020. https://www.npr.org/transcripts/174033560?storyId=174033560.

Cameron, Julia. *The Artist's Way: A Spiritual Path to Higher Creativity.* Los Angeles: TarcherPerigee, 1992.

Campbell, Joseph, with Moyers, Bill. *The Power of Myth.* New York: Doubleday, 1988.

Cassidy, Eva. "Fields of Gold." Track 8 on *Live at Blues Alley.* Eva Music, 1996. Compact disc.

Centers for Disease Control and Prevention (CDC). "1 in 3 Adults Don't Get Enough Sleep." Centers for Disease Control and Prevention. Last modified February 16, 2018. https://www.cdc.gov/media/releases/2016/p0215-enough-sleep.html.

Chron99. "Healing Waters of Mt. Clemens, Michigan." StreetDirectory.com. Accessed November 10, 2019. https://www.streetdirectory.com/travel_guide/153764/science/healing_waters_of_mt_clemens_michigan.html.

Cillizza, Chris. "Has Donald Trump Had Enough of Anthony Fauci?" *CNN Politics: The Point.* March 24, 2020. https://www.cnn.com/2020/03/24/politics/anthony-fauci-donald-trump-coronavirus-task-force/index.html.

Commission for Case Managers Certification. "About Case Management." Commission for Case Managers Certification. Accessed October 15, 2019. https://ccmcertification.org/about-ccmc/about-case-management.

Concussion. Directed by Peter Landseman. 2015. Los Angeles: Columbia Pictures, Lstar Capital, Village Roadshow Pictures, Scott Free Productions/Sony Pictures Releasing, 2016. DVD/Blu-ray.

Concussion Alliance. "Craniosacral Therapy for Concussion Symptoms." Concussion Alliance. Accessed November 10, 2019. https://www.concussionalliance.org/craniosacral-therapy.

Costandi, M. *Neuroplasticity.* Cambridge, MA: MIT Press, 2016.

Cousteau, Jacques. *The Undersea World of Jacques Cousteau.* Directed by Alan Landsburg. Aired 1968–1975. United States. 60 min.

Cowen, Alan S., and Keltner, Dacher. "Self-Report Captures 27 Distinct Categories of Emotion Bridged by Continuous Gradients." *PNAS* 114, no. 38 (September 5, 2017): E7900–E7909. https://doi.org/10.1073/pnas.1702247114.

Cozolino, Louis. *The Neuroscience of Psychotherapy: Healing the Social Brain.* 2nd ed. New York: W. W. Norton, 2010.

Denton, G. L. *Brainlash: Maximize Your Recovery from Mild Brain Injury.* New York: Demos Health, 2008.

Deutsch-Nadir, Sharon. "Capitalizing on Women's Traditional Roles in Israeli Peace Activism." Master's thesis, Fletcher School—Tufts University, 2005. http://www.isha2isha.com/wp-content/uploads/2014/02/Deutsch-Nadir_Women_roles.pdf.

Diagnostic and Statistical Manual of Mental Disorders: DSM-5. Arlington, VA: American Psychiatric Association, 2013.

Dispenza, Joe. *You Are the Placebo: Making Your Mind Matter.* Carlsbad, CA: Hay House, 2014.

Doidge, N. *The Brain That Changes Itself.* New York: Penguin, 2007.

Donohue, Amanda. "Whiplash: More Than Standard Neck Pain." American Chiropractic Association. Accessed February 4, 2016. https://www.acatoday.org/News-

Publications/ACA-News-Archive/ArtMID/5721/ArticleID/116/Whiplash-More-than-Standard-Neck-Pain.

Dyer, Wayne W. "Finding Meaning in Challenging Times." *Dr. Wayne W. Dyer Podcast.* Podcast audio. May 26, 2019. https://www.iheart.com/podcast/286-dr-wayne-w-dyer-pod-28854940/episode/dr-wayne-w-dyer-finding-43175142/.

Ehsanian, Reza. "New Treatments in Traumatic Brain Injury: A Clinical Trial of Repetitive Transcranial Magnetic Stimulation." Association of Academic Physiatrists. March 1, 2018. https://medium.com/physiatry/new-treatments-in-traumatic-brain-injury-a-clinical-trial-of-repetitive-transcranial-magnetic-929282c6b5b2.

Eidlitz-Markus, T., Shuper, A., and Amir, J. "Secondary Enuresis: Post-Traumatic Stress Disorder in Children after Car Accidents." *Israel Medical Association Journal* 2, no. 2 (2000): 135–37. https://www.ncbi.nlm.nih.gov/pubmed/10804937.

Elliott, Clark. *The Ghost in My Brain: How a Concussion Stole My Life and How the New Science of Brain Plasticity Helped Me Get It Back.* New York: Penguin, 2016.

Ellis, A., Stores, G., and Mayou, R. "Psychological Consequences of Road Traffic Accidents in Children." *European Child & Adolescent Psychiatry* 7, no. 2 (1998): 61–68.

Esty, Mary Lee, and Shifflett, C. M. *Conquering Concussion: Healing TBI Symptoms with Neurofeedback and without Drugs.* Sewickley, PA: Round Earth Publishing, 2014.

Fainaru-Wada, M., and Fainaru, S. *League of Denial: The NFL, Concussions, and the Battle for Truth.* New York: Crown Archetype, 2013.

Feinman, Jay M. *Delay, Deny, Defend: Why Insurance Companies Don't Pay Claims and What You Can Do about It.* New York: Portfolio Hardcover, 2010.

Filley, C. M. *The Behavioral Neurology of White Matter.* New York: Oxford University Press, 2001.

Finestone, H. M. *The Pain Detective: Every Ache Tells a Story—Understanding How Stress and Emotional Hurt Become Chronic Physical Pain.* Westport, CT: Praeger, 2009.

Foreman, Judy. *A Nation in Pain: Healing Our Biggest Health Problem.* New York: Oxford University Press, 2014.

Frankl, Viktor. *Man's Search for Meaning.* Boston: Beacon Press, 1959.

Fredrickson, B. L. *Positivity.* New York: Three Rivers Press, 2009.

Freud, Sigmund. *Beyond the Pleasure Principle.* New York: W. W. Norton, 1990.

———. "Remembering, Repeating, and Working-Through." In *The Standard Edition of the Complete Psychological Works of Sigmund Freud—Volume XII.* London: Hogarth Press and the Institute of Psycho-Analysis, 1964.

Furness, Penny, Vogt, Katharina, Ashe, Simon, Taylor, Sophie, Haywood-Small, Sarah, and Lawson, Kim. "What Causes Fibromyalgia: An Online Survey of Patient Perspectives." *Health Psychology Open* 5, no. 2 (July–December 2018): 20551029 18802683. Accessed September 27, 2018. https://www.ncbi.nlm.nih.gov/pmc/articles/PMC6158621.

Ganguly, K. K. "Life of M. K. Gandhi: A Message to Youth of Modern India." *Indian Journal of Medical Research* 149, Suppl 1 (January 2019): S145–51. https://www.ncbi.nlm.nih.gov/pmc/articles/PMC6515741.

Gearhart, Shannon. "Phineas Gage: American Railroad Foreman." *Encyclopedia Britannica.* https://www.britannica.com/biography/Phineas-Gage.

Gennarelli, T. A., Champion, H. R., Copes, W. S., and Sacco, W. J. "Comparison of Mortality, Morbidity, and Severity of 59,713 Head-Injured Patients with 114,447 Patients with Extracranial Injuries." *Trauma and Acute Care Surgery* 37, no. 6 (December 1994): 962–68. https://www.ncbi.nlm.nih.gov/pubmed/7996612.

Gil, Eliana. *Posttraumatic Play in Children: What Clinicians Need to Know.* New York: Guilford, 2017.

Goldberg, E. *The Executive Brain*. New York: Oxford University Press, 2001.
Gordon, M. L. *The Clinical Application of Interventional Endocrinology*. Beverly Hills, CA: Phoenix Books, 2007.
———. *Traumatic Brain Injury: A Clinical Approach to Diagnosis and Treatment: A Clinical Workbook*. Encino, CA: Millennium Health Centers, 2016.
Gordon, Mark, and Marr, Andrew. "A Paradigm Shift in the Diagnosis and Treatment of Symptomatic Brain Injury." Millennium Neuro-Regenerative Centers. Last modified September 2018. http://www.tbimedlegal.com/sitebuildercontent/sitebuilderfiles/WhitePaper.pdf.
Greenough, Jeanie. *A Year of Beautiful Thoughts*. Alcester, UK: Read, 2007.
Hadanny, A., Abbott, Stefanie, Suzin, Gil, Bechor, Yair, and Efrati, Shai. "Effect of Hyperbaric Oxygen Therapy on Chronic Neurocognitive Deficits of Post-Traumatic Brain Injury Patients: Retrospective Analysis." *BMJ Open*. Last modified 2018. https://bmjopen.bmj.com/content/8/9/e023387.
Hakomi Institute of California. "Method and Process." Hakomi Institute of California. Accessed November 18, 2019. https://www.hakomica.org/about-hakomi/method-process.
Hamilton, Scott. "'The Only Disability in Life Is a Bad Attitude.' Meme." Fabric of Digital Life, 2012.
Hanscom, D. *Back in Control: A Surgeon's Roadmap Out of Chronic Pain*. Seattle, WA: Vertus Press, 2017.
Harrell, Kelley S. *Gift of the Dreamtime—Reader's Companion*. Fuquay-Varina, NC: Soul Intent Arts, 2014.
Hay, Louise. "Real Way to Practice Self-Love." YouTube video, 9:59. Posted by Guided Meditation and More with Aditii. March 27, 2018. https://youtu.be/m8gHWQCZQD4.
Heller, D. P., and Heller, L. *Crash Course: A Self-Healing Guide to Auto Accident Trauma & Recovery*. Berkeley, CA: North Atlantic Books, 2001.
Hemingway, Ernest. *By-Line: Ernest Hemingway: Selected Articles and Dispatches of Four Decades*. Edited by William White. New York, Scribner, 1998.
———. *A Farewell to Arms*. New York: Scribner, 1995.
Herman, Judith Lewis. *Trauma and Recovery: The Aftermath of Violence—from Domestic Abuse to Political Terror*. New York: Basic Books, 1997.
Hickling, E. J., and Blanchard, E. B., eds. *The International Handbook of Road Traffic Accidents & Psychological Trauma: Current Understanding, Treatment and Law*. Amsterdam, Netherlands: Elsevier, 1999.
———. *Overcoming the Trauma of Your Motor Vehicle Accident: A Cognitive-Behavioral Treatment Program: Therapist Guide*. New York: Oxford University Press, 2006.
Hil, William Ely. "My Wife and My Mother-in-Law." Cartoon drawing. *Puck*, 1915.
Holmes, C. S., ed. *Psychoneuroendocrinology: Brain, Behavior, and Hormonal Interactions*. New York: Springer-Verlag, 2014.
Houry, Debra. "New Data Show Growing Complexity of Drug Overdose Deaths in America." CDC. Accessed December 21, 2018. https://www.cdc.gov/media/releases/2018/p1221-complexity-drug-overdose.html.
Howard, Michael E. *Managing Chronic Pain, Part 1: Types of Pain & Pain Pathways*. Concord, CA: Institute for Natural Resources, 2015.
Howard, Timothy. "Should I Still Go See a Doctor after a Minor Car Accident." Dr. Harry W. Brown's Arrowhead Clinic. Accessed September 3, 2019. https://www.arrowheadclinic.com/category/blog/should-i-still-go-see-a-doctor-after-a-minor-car-accident#see-a-doctor.

Insurance Institute for Highway Safety. "Cellular Phone Use and Texting While Driving Laws." National Conference of State Legislatures. May 29, 2019. https://www.ncsl. org/research/transportation/cellular-phone-use-and-texting-while-driving-laws.aspx.

"Interview with Dr. John Sarno on His Book *The Divided Mind*." YouTube video, 26:26. Posted by Paul Mabry. April 29, 2017. Accessed November 16, 2019. https:// youtu.be/mzOBa-t6Vcw.

James, William. *The Principles of Psychology*. New York: Henry Holt, 1890.

Jamo, E = mc. "Humpty Dumpty and the Second Law of Thermodynamics." *EMCJamo blogspot*. Accessed May 30, 2019. http://emcjamo.blogspot.com/search?q=humpty+ dumpty.

Jansen, Bart. "Millennial Drivers Are Highway Hazards, Survey Shows." *USA Today*. February 15, 2017. https://www.usatoday.com/story/news/2017/02/15/millennial-drivers-highway-hazards-survey-shows/97888336.

Jung, C. G. *Collected Works of C. G. Jung*. Vol. 7. Princeton, NJ: Princeton University Press, 2014.

Kenney, K. S., and Fanciullo, L. M. "Automobile Air Bags: Friend or Foe? A Case of Air Bag–Associated Ocular Trauma and Related Literature Review." *Optometry* 76, no. 7 (2005): 382–86. Accessed June 2, 2019. https://www.ncbi.nlm.nih.gov/ pubmed/16038865.

Keppel-Benson, J. M., Ollendick, T. H., and Benson, M. J. "Post-Traumatic Stress in Children Following Motor Vehicle Accidents." *Journal of Child Psychology and Psychiatry* 43, no. 2 (February 2002): 203–12. First published March 12, 2002. https://doi.org/10.1111/1469-7610.00013.

King, N. S. "Post-Traumatic Stress Disorder and Head Injury as a Dual Diagnosis: 'Islands' of Memory as a Mechanism." *Journal of Neurology, Neurosurgery and Psychiatry* 62, no. 1 (1997): 82–84.

Kizorek, Bill. "Investigation of Psychological Claims." In *The Insurer's Handbook of Psychological Injury Claims*, edited by David R. Price and P. R. Lees-Haley. Seattle, WA: Claims Books, 1995.

Klonoff, P. *Psychotherapy after Brain Injury*. New York: Guilford, 2010.

Kohn, David. "Could Hyperbaric Treatment Heal the Brain?" *Washington Post*. January 27, 2018. https://www.washingtonpost.com/national/health-science/could-hyperbar ic-treatment-heal-the-brain/2018/01/26/90b3acfa-df87-11e7-8679-a9728984779c_ story.html.

Kotler, S. *The Rise of Superman: Decoding the Science of Ultimate Human Perfor- mance*. London: Quercus, 2014.

Kotler, S., and Wheal, J. *Stealing Fire*. New York: HarperCollins, 2017.

Kramer, M. B., Shattuck, T. G., and Charnock, D. R. "Traumatic Hearing Loss Follow- ing Air-Bag Inflation." *New England Journal of Medicine* 337 (1997): 574–75. Ac- cessed October 4, 2019. https://www.nejm.org/doi/full/10.1056/NEJM199708213 370817.

Kübler-Ross, E. *On Grief and Grieving: Finding the Meaning of Grief through the Five Stages of Loss*. New York, Scribner, 2007.

Laskis, J. M. *Concussion*. New York: Random House, 2015.

Lawcore. "Car Accident Statistics." Lawcore.com. Accessed November 19, 2019. http:// www.lawcore.com/car-accident/statistics.html.

Leng, G. *The Heart of the Brain: The Hypothalamus and Its Hormones*. Cambridge, MA: MIT Press, 2018.

Levine, P. A., with Frederick, A. *Waking the Tiger: Healing Trauma*. Berkeley, CA: North Atlantic Books, 1997.

Lewis, Michael D. *When Brains Collide*. New York: Lioncrest, 2016.

Lindy, J. D. "The Trauma Membrane and Other Clinical Concepts Derived from Psychotherapeutic Work with Survivors of Natural Disasters." *Psychiatric Annals*

15, no. 3 (1985): 153–60. Last modified March 1, 1985. https://doi.org/10.3928/0048-5713-19850301-06.

Lino, Catarina. "Broaden-and-Build Theory of Positive Emotions." PositivePsychology.com. March 7, 2019. https://positivepsychology.com/broaden-build-theory.

———. "Positive Psychology: An Introduction." PositivePsychology.com. Accessed November 11, 2019. https://positivepsychology.com/positive-psychology-an-introduction-summary.

Lipton, Bruce H. *The Biology of Belief: Unleashing the Power of Consciousness, Matter & Miracles.* Carlsbad, CA: Hay House, 2008.

Luehrs, Adam. "Seven Problems Self-Driving Cars Need to Overcome." Smith's Lawyers. Accessed August 13, 2018. https://www.smithslawyers.com.au/post/self-driving-car-problems.

Luskin, F. *Forgive for Good.* New York: HarperCollins, 2003.

MacLennan, Carol A. "From Accident to Crash: The Auto Industry and the Politics of Injury," *Medical Anthropology Quarterly / International Journal for the Analysis of Health* 2, no. 3 (September 1988): 233–30. https://doi.org/10.1525/maq.1988.2.3.02a00040.

Malek, M., Guyer, B., and Lescohier, I. "The Epidemiology and Prevention of Child Pedestrian Injury." *Accident Analysis & Prevention* 22, no. 4 (August 1990): 301–13. https://www.sciencedirect.com/science/article/abs/pii/000145759090046N.

Marks, Tracey I. *Master Your Sleep: Proven Methods Simplified.* Minneapolis, MN: Bascom Hill, 2011.

Markus, Donalee. Foreword to *The Ghost in My Brain*, by C. Elliott. New York: Penguin, 2016.

Marr, A., and Marr, A. *Tales from the Blast Factory: A Brain Injured Special Forces Green Beret's Journey Back from the Brink.* New York: Morgan James, 2018.

Mason, Michael P. *Head Cases: Stories of Brain Injury and Its Aftermath.* New York: Farrar, Straus & Giroux, 2008.

Maté, Gabor. *In the Realm of the Hungry Ghosts: Close Encounters with Addiction.* Berkeley, CA: North Atlantic Books, 2010.

Mayo Clinic. "Hypnosis." Mayo Clinic. Accessed October 3, 2019. https://www.mayoclinic.org/tests-procedures/hypnosis/about/pac-20394405.

Mayo Clinic Staff. "Whiplash." Mayo Clinic. February 5, 2020. Accessed March 17, 2020. https://www.mayoclinic.org/diseases-conditions/whiplash/symptoms-causes/syc-20378921.

McCartt, Anne T. "100 Deadliest Road Days." *Her Highway* (blog). May 18, 2012. http://www.herhighway.com/blog/100-deadliest-road-days.

McCrea, M. A. *Mild Traumatic Brain Injury and Postconcussion Syndrome.* New York: Oxford University Press, 2008.

McEwan, Ian. *Atonement: A Novel.* New York: Anchor Books, 2007.

Meehan, William P., III. *Kids, Sports, and Concussions: A Guide for Coaches and Parents.* Santa Barbara, CA: Praeger, 2011.

Melzack, R., and Wall, P. D. *The Challenge of Pain.* New York: Penguin, 2008.

———. "Pain Mechanisms: A New Theory." *Science* 150, no. 3699 (November 19, 1965): 971–79. https://www.ncbi.nlm.nih.gov/pubmed/5320816.

Merskey, H., and Bogduk, N. *Classification of Chronic Pain: Description of Chronic Pain Syndromes and Definition of Pain Terms.* Seattle, WA: IASP Press, 1994.

Migraine Resources Center. "When to Suspect a CSF Leak in Patients with Headache." *Neurology Reviews.* Accessed September 2017. https://www.mdedge.com/neurology/migraineresourcecenter/article/132780/headache-migraine/when-suspect-csf-leak.

Miller, Korin. "What Is Naloxone?" *Women's Health Magazine.* March 22, 2018. https://www.womenshealthmag.com/health/a19562876/what-is-naloxone.

Mirza, K. A. H., Bhadrinath, B. R., Goodyer, I. M., and Gilmour, C. "Post-Traumatic Stress Disorder in Children and Adolescents Following Road Traffic Accidents." *British Journal of Psychiatry* 172, no. 5 (May 1998): 443–47. Published online January 3, 2018. https://doi.org/10.1192/bjp.172.5.443.

Mohammed, S., and Yu, J. S. "Platelet-Rich Plasma Injections: An Emerging Therapy for Chronic Discogenic Low Back Pain." *Journal of Spine Surgery* 4, no. 1 (March 2018): 115–22. Accessed March 4, 2018. https://www.ncbi.nlm.nih.gov/pmc/articles/PMC5911760.

Morris, David J. *The Evil Hours: A Biography of Post-Traumatic Stress Disorder.* Rancho Cucomonga, CA: Houghton Mifflin Harcourt, 2015.

My Beautiful Broken Brain. Directed by Sophie Robinson and Lotje Sodderland. 2014. United Kingdom: Sophie Robinson/IDIFA, Netflix, 2016.

Nandapalan, V., Watson, I. D., and Swift, A. C. "Beta-2-Transferrin and Cerebrospinal Fluid Rhinorrhea." *Clinical Otolaryngology and Allied Sciences* 2, no. 3 (June 1996): 259–64. Accessed September 22, 2019. https://doi.org/10.1111/j.1365-2273.1996.tb01737.x.

Nantulya, Vinand M., and Reich, Michael R. (Harvard Center for Population and Development Studies). "The Neglected Epidemic: Road Traffic Injuries in Developing Countries." *BMJ* 324, no. 7346 (May 11, 2002): 1139–41. https://www.ncbi.nlm.nih.gov/pubmed/12003888.

National Highway Transportation Administration. "Drug and Alcohol Crash Risk Study." National Highway Transportation Administration. Last modified August 13, 2018. https://www.nhtsa.gov/behavioral-research/drug-and-alcohol-crash-risk-study.

National Institute of Mental Health. "Post-Traumatic Stress Disorder." National Institute of Mental Health. May 2019. Accessed November 19, 2019. https://www.nimh.nih.gov/health/topics/post-traumatic-stress-disorder-ptsd/index.shtml.

National Safety Council. "Drowsy Driving Is Impaired Driving." National Safety Council. Accessed October 12, 2019. https://www.nsc.org/Portals/0/Documents/Fatigue%20Documents/Fact-Sheets/Drowsy-Driving-Problem-and-Statistics.pdf.

———. "For the First Time, We're More Likely to Die from Accidental Opioid Overdose than Motor Vehicle Crash." National Safety Council: In the Newsroom. January 14, 2019. https://www.nsc.org/in-the-newsroom/for-the-first-time-were-more-likely-to-die-from-accidental-opioid-overdose-than-motor-vehicle-crash.

———. "Motor Vehicle Deaths Estimated to Have Dropped 2% in 2019." National Safety Council. https://www.nsc.org/road-safety/safety-topics/fatality-estimates.

———. "Your Odds of Dying from an Accidental Opioid Overdose Continue to Be Greater than Dying in a Motor-Vehicle Crash." Injury Facts. Accessed March 18, 2020. https://injuryfacts.nsc.org/all-injuries/preventable-death-overview/odds-of-dying.

Nelson, January. "A List of Emotions and Facial Expressions." Thought Catalog. Last updated July 29, 2018. Accessed April 2, 2020. https://thoughtcatalog.com/january-nelson/2018/06/list-of-emotions.

Newton, John, and Cowper, William. "Amazing Grace." In *Olney Hymns*, Church of England, 1779.

Niebuhr, Karl Paul Reinhold. "The Serenity Prayer." *AA Grapevine.* January 1950, 6–7.

Nigro, Samuel A. *The Soul of the Earth.* Rev. ed. St. Louis, MO: Central Bureau, 2012.

Ohki, Masafumi, Ishikawa, Jyunichi, and Tahara, Atsushi. "Sensorineural Hearing Loss Due to Air Bag Deployment." *Case Reports in Otolaryngology* (2012): 203714. https://www.ncbi.nlm.nih.gov/pmc/articles/PMC3420767.

Omalu, B., with Tabb, M. *Truth Doesn't Have a Side: My Alarming Discovery about the Danger of Contact Sports.* Grand Rapids, MI: Zondervan, 2017.

Osborn, C. L. *Over My Head: A Doctor's Own Story of Head Injury from the Inside Looking Out.* Kansas City, MO: Andrews McMeel, 1998.

Oxford New Desk Dictionary, 3rd edition. New York: The Berkley Publishing Group, 2009.

Page, D. W. *Body Trauma: A Writer's Guide to Wounds and Injuries.* 2nd ed. Lake Forest, CA: Behler, 2006.

Park, Andrea. "Lady Gaga Describes What Her PTSD Symptoms Feel Like: 'My Whole Body Goes into a Spasm.'" *Self.* September 11, 2018. https://www.self.com/story/lady-gaga-discusses-chronic-pain.

Parker, R. S. "The Spectrum of Emotional Distress and Personality Changes after Minor Head Injury Incurred in a Motor Vehicle Accident." *Brain Injury* 10, no. 4 (1996): 287–302.

Parker, R. S., and Rosenblum, A. "IQ Loss and Personality Dysfunctions after Mild Head Injury Incurred in a Motor Vehicle Accident." *Journal of Clinical Psychology* 52, no. 1 (1996): 32–43. https://onlinelibrary.wiley.com/doi/10.1002/%28SICI %291097-4679%28199601%2952%3A1%3C32%3A%3AAID-JCLP5%3E3.0. CO%3B2-Y.

Payne, Roman. *Wanderess Quotes and Other Poems.* Boca Raton, FL: Aesthete Press, 2017.

Pilates, J. H., and Miller, W. J. *Return to Life through Contrology: Presentation Dynamics.* Locust Valley, NY: J. J. Augustin, 1945.

Pintar, Frank, Yoganandan, Narayan, and Gennarelli, Thomas. "Airbag Effectiveness on Brain Trauma in Frontal Crashes." *Association for the Advancement of Automotive Medicine* 44 (2000): 149–69. Accessed August 6, 2019. https://www.researchgate.net/publication/11789971_Airbag_Effectiveness_on_Brain_Trauma_in_Frontal_Crashes.

Prechtel, Martin. *Secrets of the Talking Jaguar: A Mayan Shaman's Journey to the Heart of the Indigenous Soul.* New York: TarcherPerigee, 1998.

———. *Secrets of the Talking Jaguar: Memoirs from the Living Heart of a Mayan Village.* New York: TarcherPerigee, 1999.

Price, D. R., and Lees-Haley, P. R., eds. *The Insurer's Handbook of Psychological Injury Claims.* Seattle, WA: Claims Books, 1995.

Quinones, S. *Dreamland: The True Tale of America's Opiate Epidemic.* London: Bloomsbury, 2015.

Red Asphalt. Produced by the California Highway Patrol, 1964–2006. Film series.

Rees, R. J. *Interrupted Lives: Rehabilitation and Learning Following Brain Injury.* East Hawthorn, Australia: IP Communications, 2005.

Rendon, J. *The New Science of Post-Traumatic Growth.* New York: Touchstone, 2015.

Rice, Norman B. *Pass It On.* Accessed September 3, 2018. https://www.passiton.com/inspirational-quotes/4813-dare-to-reach-out-your-hand-into-the-darkness.

Rio, L. M. *The Hormone Factor in Mental Health.* London: Jessica Kingsley, 2014.

Rizzo, M., and Tranel, D., eds. *Head Injury and Postconcussive Syndrome.* London: Churchill Livingston, 1996.

RoadPeace. "About RoadPeace." RoadPeace. Accessed November 21, 2019. http://www.roadpeace.org/about-roadpeace.

Rosenberg, S. *Accessing the Healing Power of the Vagus Nerve: Self-Help Exercises for Anxiety, Depression, Trauma, and Autism.* Berkeley, CA: North Atlantic Books, 2017.

Rugg, R. M., and Chester, S. K. *Effective Psychotherapy for Individuals with Brain Injury.* New York: Guilford, 2014.

Saperstein, R., and Saperstein, D. *Surviving an Auto Accident: A Guide to Your Physical, Economic and Emotional Recovery.* Tucson, AZ: Pathfinder, 1994.

Sarno, John. *Mind over Back Pain.* New York: Berkley Books, 1999.

Schubiner, Howard, and Betzold, Michael. *Unlearn Your Pain.* 3rd ed. Pleasant Ridge, MI: Mind Body Publishing, 2013.

Schweitzer, Albert. *On the Edge of the Primeval Forest*. 2.02 ed. Acton, MA: Actonian Press, 2010.

Seligman, M. E. P. *Flourish*. New York: Atria Paperback, 2011.

Selye, H. *Stress*. Montreal: Acta Medical, 1950.

Senelick, Richard C., and Dougherty, K. *Living with Brain Injury: A Guide for Families*. Independence, KY: Delmar Cengage Learning, 2001.

Sherin, J. E., and Nemeroff, C. B. "Post-Traumatic Stress Disorder: The Neurobiological Impact of Psychological Trauma." *Dialogues in Clinical Neuroscience* 13, no. 3 (September 2011): 263–78. https://www.ncbi.nlm.nih.gov/pmc/articles/PMC318 2008.

Sherry, M. *If I Only Had a Brain: Deconstructing Brain Injury*. New York: Routledge, 2006.

Shorter, E., and Fink, M. *Endocrine Psychiatry*. New York: Oxford University Press, 2010.

Sinas Dramis Law Firm. "Michigan's No-Fault Allowable Expense Benefits." Sinas Dramis. Accessed March 18, 2020. https://sinasdramis.com/michigan-auto-accident-attorneys/no-fault-allowable-expense-benefits.

Sinas, G. T., Sinas, S. H., and Sinas, T. G. *The Michigan Auto No-Fault Law: Your Rights & Benefits: A Detailed Guide for Patients and Providers*. 8th ed. Grand Rapids, MI: Sinas Dramis Law Firm, 2017.

Smith, Timothy C. *Crashproof Your Kids: Make Your Teen a Safer, Smarter Driver*. New York: Fireside, 2006.

Sosin, D. M., Sacks, J. J., and Holmgreen, P. "Head Injury—Associated Deaths from Motorcycle Crashes: Relationship to Helmet-Use Laws." *JAMA* 264, no. 18 (1990): 2395–99. doi:10.1001/jama.1990.03450180059029.

Spinal CSF Leak Foundation. "Diagnosis." Spinal CSF Leak Foundation. Accessed September 22, 2019. https://spinalcsfleak.org/about-spinal-csf-leaks/diagnosis.

Surviving Traumatic Brain Injury. "Fatigue and the Spoon Theory." Surviving Traumatic Brain Injury. Accessed November 2, 2019. https://survivingtraumaticbraininjury.com/2015/03/23/brain-injury-resources-fatigue-and-the-spoon-theory.

Swanson, K. L. *I'll Carry the Fork: Recovering a Life after Brain Injury*. Scotts Valley, CA: Rising Star Press, 2003.

Sweeton, Jennifer. "Here's Your Brain on Trauma." *Jennifer Sweeton Blog*. February 23, 2017. https://www.jennifersweeton.com/blog/2017/3/14/heres-your-brain-on-trauma.

Tafur, Joseph. *The Fellowship of the River: A Medical Doctor's Exploration into Traditional Amazonian Plant Medicine*. Phoenix, AZ: Espiritu Books, 2017.

Takasaki, J., Arai, K., Ando, M., Nagahama, T., Fukuda, A., Ami, K., Kurokawa, T. et al. "Examination of the Effect of Anesthesia on Radiofrequency Ablation of Hepatocellular Carcinoma—a Patient Survey on Radiofrequency Ablation." *Gan To KagakuRyoho* 39, no. 12 (November 2012): 1843–45. https://www.ncbi.nlm.nih.gov/pubmed/23267905.

Taylor, Martin T. *My Neck Hurts! Nonsurgical Treatments for Neck and Upper Back Pain*. Baltimore: Johns Hopkins University Press, 2010.

Terr, Lenore. *Too Scared to Cry: How Trauma Affects Children and Ultimately Us All*. Repr. ed. New York: Basic Books, 1992.

Truman, Karol K. *Feelings Buried Alive Never Die*. Rev. ed. Saint George, UT: Olympus Distributing, 1995.

Unknown. "Rabbit-Duck Illusion." Cartoon drawing. *Fliegende Blätter*, 1892.

UNM Department of Psychiatry Grand Rounds. "UNM Department of Psychiatry Grand Rounds: Lenore Terr, M.D." YouTube video. 1:25:52. May 22, 2013. https://youtu.be/czA5X7eTeos.

U.S. Department of Veterans Affairs. "PTSD Basics." U.S. Department of Veterans Affairs: PTSD: National Center for PTSD. Accessed July 15, 2019. https://www.ptsd.va.gov/understand/what/ptsd_basics.asp.

Vanderbeken, Ines, and Kerckhofs, Eric. "A Systematic Review of the Effect of Physical Exercise on Cognition in Stroke and Traumatic Brain Injury Patients." *NeuroRehabilitation* 40 (2017): 33–48, https://pdfs.semanticscholar.org/d636/0a421f 93dc075e97e5052dc13c1094bccbd9.pdf.

Van der Kolk, Bessel A. *The Body Keeps the Score: Brain, Mind, and Body in the Healing of Trauma.* Morrisville, NC: Lulu Press, 2019.

Vasterling, J. J., Bryant, R., and Keane, T., eds. *PTSD and Mild Traumatic Brain Injury.* New York: Guilford, 2012.

Virgin, J. J. *Miracle Mindset.* New York: Gallery Books, 2017.

Wang, Yong Tai, Huang, Guoyuan, Duke, Gloria, and Yang, Yi. "Tai-Chi, Yoga, and Qigong as Mind-Body Exercises." *Evidence-Based Complementary and Alternate Medicine,* Last modified January 5, 2017, https://www.hindawi.com/journals/ecam/ 2017/8763913.

Weisz, Robert. "Attention Is Love." Mindfulness Based Emotional Processing. Accessed November 2, 2019. https://mindfulnessbasedemotionalprocessing.com/new-client-forms.

———. "Episode 03 P2W: Brainspotting." YouTube video, 27:07. Posted by Dr. Christian O'Neill. March 16, 2013. Accessed September 5, 2019. https://youtu.be/ 53NeelMCW24.

Wim Hof Method. "Advantages of the Wim Hof Breathing Exercises" Wim Hof Method. Accessed November 5, 2019. https://www.wimhofmethod.com/breathing-exercises.

Wolkowitz, O. M., and Rothschild, A. J. *Psychoneuroendocrinology: The Scientific Basis for Clinical Practice.* Washington, DC: American Psychiatric Publishing, 2003.

Woodruff, Lee, and Woodruff, Bob. *In an Instant: A Family's Journey of Love and Healing.* New York: Random House, 2008.

World Health Organization (WHO). "10 Facts about Road Safety." *World Health Organization: Newsroom.* Accessed August 2, 2019. https://www.who.int/news-room/ facts-in-pictures/detail/road-safety.

———. "Global Status Report on Road Safety 2018: Summary." World Health Organization. Accessed December 2018. https://www.who.int/violence_injury_prevention/ road_safety_status/2018/en.

———. "Road Traffic Injuries." *World Health Organization: Newsroom.* Last modified February 7, 2020. https://www.who.int/en/news-room/fact-sheets/detail/road-traffic-injuries.

Young, B. H., and Blake, D. D., eds. *Group Treatments for Post-Traumatic Stress Disorder.* New York: Brunner Mazel, 1999.

Zender, J. F. *The New Normal. Psychology Today Blog.* 2019.

———. "No-Fault Insurance Coverage That Matters." *Detroit News: Opinion.* February 17, 2016.

———. "Omega-3s in the Treatment of Posttraumatic Brain Injury." *Psychology Today: The New Normal* (blog). December 27, 2018. Accessed April 1, 2020. https:// www.psychologytoday.com/us/blog/the-new-normal/201812/omega-3s-in-the-treatment-posttraumatic-brain-injury.

INDEX

AA. *See* Alcoholics Anonymous
accidents: with children pedestrians,
164; common injuries and,
xxx–xxxii, 2, 16, 17, 18–22, 23,
42–43, 62; Covid-19 pandemic and,
xxi; distracted driving and,
143–144, 168; drunk driving and,
136, 137, 141–143, 144–145, 148,
164, 168; economics of, xx, 76, 115,
128, 158, 169; emergency
departments after, 138–139, 140; for
emergency medical personnel,
138–139, 139–140, 141; emotions
after, 23, 80; fatalities and, 2, 130,
142, 162, 164, 169; global concerns
for, 157–159; grief after, 77, 91,
124, 154; marijuana and, 145–146;
memory of, 76, 127–128, 131,
136–137; in Namibia, 162–163;
with pedestrians, 49, 162; preaccident trauma and, 7–8;
prevention of, 135–136, 143–149,
158–159, 159, 161–162, 167, 169;
as public health crisis, xxix, 157;
quality of life after, xx, xxvii, xxx,
xxxi, 2, 20, 23, 24, 30, 59, 63; from
risky driving behaviors, 168–169;
statistics for, 130, 158, 161–162,

164–165, 166–167, 169; suicidal
thoughts after, 18, 24
ACPA. *See* American Chronic Pain
Association
acting out, 132
addiction, 12, 61, 68, 69–70, 88
adrenaline, 98, 139
advice, for caregivers, family and
friends of survivors, 123–126, 134
aggression, 2–3, 3, 8
airbags, 19, 75, 78
airplanes, 51
alcohol. *See* drunk driving
Alcoholics Anonymous (AA), 81, 101
alternatives, for pain management,
61–62, 70–72
"Amazing Grace" (song), 91
American Chiropractic Association, 17
American Chronic Pain Association
(ACPA), 60
American Psychiatric Association
(APA), 29
American Sleep Foundation, 169
anger, 24–25, 71, 90, 107, 107–108,
123, 128, 129, 143, 154
anxiety, xxvii, xxxii, 2, 3, 12, 15,
23–24, 62, 96, 98, 103–104, 128,
163–164, 165; depression and, xi,

ABOUT THE AUTHOR

James F. Zender, PhD, is a clinical and forensic psychologist, certified brain injury specialist, and certified traumatologist. His *Psychology Today* blog, *The New Normal*, made Heathline's list of the Best Traumatic Brain Injury Blogs of 2019. Zender was the founding director of the Center for the Prevention and Treatment of Psychological Trauma at Detroit Receiving Hospital and University Health Center and a full-time affiliate instructor in psychiatry at Wayne State University School of Medicine. For the past 15 years, his private practice in the Detroit Metro Area has focused on vehicular trauma injury recovery. He has lectured at the World Psychiatric Association, Harvard Medical School, the International Society of Traumatic Stress Studies, and the American Psychological Association.

ABOUT THE AUTHOR

James F. Zender, PhD, is a clinical and forensic psychologist, certified brain injury specialist, and certified traumatologist. His *Psychology Today* blog, *The New Normal*, made Heathline's list of the Best Traumatic Brain Injury Blogs of 2019. Zender was the founding director of the Center for the Prevention and Treatment of Psychological Trauma at Detroit Receiving Hospital and University Health Center and a full-time affiliate instructor in psychiatry at Wayne State University School of Medicine. For the past 15 years, his private practice in the Detroit Metro Area has focused on vehicular trauma injury recovery. He has lectured at the World Psychiatric Association, Harvard Medical School, the International Society of Traumatic Stress Studies, and the American Psychological Association.

CPSIA information can be obtained
at www.ICGtesting.com
Printed in the USA
BVHW042112180920
589015BV00007B/15